P9-EKY-857

**INTRODUCING
ISSUES WITH
OPPOSING
VIEWPOINTS**®

Oceans

Lauri S. Friedman, *Book Editor*

GREENHAVEN PRESS
A part of Gale, Cengage Learning

GALE
CENGAGE Learning™

Detroit • New York • San Francisco • New Haven, Conn • Waterville, Maine • London

Christine Nasso, *Publisher*
Elizabeth Des Chenes, *Managing Editor*

LIBRARY OF CONGRESS CATALOGING-IN-PUBLICATION DATA

Oceans / Lauri S. Friedman, book editor.
    p. cm. -- (Introducing issues with opposing viewpoints)
  Includes bibliographical references and index.
  ISBN 978-0-7377-5200-7 (hardcover)
  1. Ocean. 2. Marine pollution. 3. Marine resources conservation. I. Friedman, Lauri S.
  GC21.O273 2011
  551.46--dc22

                                                                    2011005910

Printed in the United States of America
1 2 3 4 5 6 7 15 14 13 12 11

Contents

Foreword   5

Introduction   7

Chapter 1: How Are Oceans Changing?

1. Oceans Are Warming   11
   Mary Ann Whitley

2. Oceans Are Cooling   16
   Lorne Gunter

3. Ocean Levels Are Rising   21
   Rob Young and Orrin Pilkey

4. Ocean Levels Are Not Rising   30
   Marc Sheppard

5. Oceans Are Becoming Dangerously Acidic   37
   Natural Resources Defense Council

6. The Threat of Ocean Acidification Is Exaggerated   43
   Tim Ball

Chapter 2: What Are the Most Significant Threats to Oceans?

1. Overfishing Is a Serious Threat to Oceans   50
   Daniel Pauly

2. The Threat of Overfishing Has Been Exaggerated   57
   Nancy Gaines

3. Fish Farming Threatens Ocean Fish Stocks   65
   Coastal Alliance for Aquaculture Reform

4. Fish Farming Need Not Threaten Ocean Fish Stocks   73
   Global Agenda

5. Plastic Waste in the Oceans Poses a Serious Threat   79
   Ed Cumming

6. The Threat from Plastic Waste in the Oceans
   Has Been Exaggerated   86
   Martin Robbins

7. Noise Pollution Is a Serious Threat to Marine Mammals   93
   International Fund for Animal Welfare

Chapter 3: How Should Oceans Be Protected?

1. Deepwater Oil Drilling Should Be Banned   102
   Matthew Daly

2. Deepwater Oil Drilling Should Not Be Banned   107
   Jane Wardell and Jennifer Quinn

3. Protecting Fish Populations Will Solve the
   Overfishing Crisis   112
   John Hocevar and Jeremy Jackson

4. The Overfishing Crisis Is a Myth   117
   Don Hansen

Facts About Oceans   122
Organizations to Contact   126
For Further Reading   133
Index   138
Picture Credits   143

Foreword

I ndulging in a wide spectrum of ideas, beliefs, and perspectives is a critical cornerstone of democracy. After all, it is often debates over differences of opinion, such as whether to legalize abortion, how to treat prisoners, or when to enact the death penalty, that shape our society and drive it forward. Such diversity of thought is frequently regarded as the hallmark of a healthy and civilized culture. As the Reverend Clifford Schutjer of the First Congregational Church in Mansfield, Ohio, declared in a 2001 sermon, "Surrounding oneself with only like-minded people, restricting what we listen to or read only to what we find agreeable is irresponsible. Refusing to entertain doubts once we make up our minds is a subtle but deadly form of arrogance." With this advice in mind, Introducing Issues with Opposing Viewpoints books aim to open readers' minds to the critically divergent views that comprise our world's most important debates.

Introducing Issues with Opposing Viewpoints simplifies for students the enormous and often overwhelming mass of material now available via print and electronic media. Collected in every volume is an array of opinions that captures the essence of a particular controversy or topic. Introducing Issues with Opposing Viewpoints books embody the spirit of nineteenth-century journalist Charles A. Dana's axiom: "Fight for your opinions, but do not believe that they contain the whole truth, or the only truth." Absorbing such contrasting opinions teaches students to analyze the strength of an argument and compare it to its opposition. From this process readers can inform and strengthen their own opinions, or be exposed to new information that will change their minds. Introducing Issues with Opposing Viewpoints is a mosaic of different voices. The authors are statesmen, pundits, academics, journalists, corporations, and ordinary people who have felt compelled to share their experiences and ideas in a public forum. Their words have been collected from newspapers, journals, books, speeches, interviews, and the Internet, the fastest growing body of opinionated material in the world.

Introducing Issues with Opposing Viewpoints shares many of the well-known features of its critically acclaimed parent series, Opposing Viewpoints. The articles are presented in a pro/con format, allowing readers to absorb divergent perspectives side by side. Active reading questions preface each viewpoint, requiring the student to approach the material thoughtfully and carefully. Useful charts, graphs, and cartoons supplement each article. A thorough introduction provides readers with crucial background on an issue. An annotated bibliography points the reader toward articles, books, and websites that contain additional information on the topic. An appendix of organizations to contact contains a wide variety of charities, nonprofit organizations, political groups, and private enterprises that each hold a position on the issue at hand. Finally, a comprehensive index allows readers to locate content quickly and efficiently.

Introducing Issues with Opposing Viewpoints is also significantly different from Opposing Viewpoints. As the series title implies, its presentation will help introduce students to the concept of opposing viewpoints and learn to use this material to aid in critical writing and debate. The series' four-color, accessible format makes the books attractive and inviting to readers of all levels. In addition, each viewpoint has been carefully edited to maximize a reader's understanding of the content. Short but thorough viewpoints capture the essence of an argument. A substantial, thought-provoking essay question placed at the end of each viewpoint asks the student to further investigate the issues raised in the viewpoint, compare and contrast two authors' arguments, or consider how one might go about forming an opinion on the topic at hand. Each viewpoint contains sidebars that include at-a-glance information and handy statistics. A Facts About section located in the back of the book further supplies students with relevant facts and figures.

Following in the tradition of the Opposing Viewpoints series, Greenhaven Press continues to provide readers with invaluable exposure to the controversial issues that shape our world. As John Stuart Mill once wrote: "The only way in which a human being can make some approach to knowing the whole of a subject is by hearing what can be said about it by persons of every variety of opinion and studying all modes in which it can be looked at by every character of mind. No wise man ever acquired his wisdom in any mode but this." It is to this principle that Introducing Issues with Opposing Viewpoints books are dedicated.

Introduction

S harks and humans have long had a tenuous relationship. Feared for decades as the world's most vicious predators, shark populations have dwindled in recent years at an alarming rate, and now, by most estimates, have more to fear from humans than vice versa. On average, there are only about sixty-five shark attacks worldwide each year, and just a few of these are fatal. Sharks and their habitat are under multiple threats, however, including overfishing; shark finning (when they are hunted for their fins, a delicacy in some Asian nations); death from nets (when sharks are caught in nets intended for other fish, called bycatch); global warming; and more. Efforts to protect sharks have increased curiosity about them, which has resulted in a controversial industry known as "shark tourism." With devout supporters and vehement opponents, shark tourism is emblematic of the delicate tension between ocean conservationism and commercialism.

Billed as a thrilling way to see the world's most fearsome predator up close, shark tourism, or shark cage diving, typically involves boating to an area off the coast; baiting the water with a grisly soup of fish guts and blood called "chum"; putting on scuba gear and immersing oneself in a metal, bite-resistant cage suspended a few feet below the surface of the water; and waiting for predators to circle. For the chance to see sharks close-up in their natural environment, tourists travel to Hawaii, South Africa, the Bahamas, and other exotic locations. They pay hundreds of dollars per outing and come face-to-face with great white, tiger, and others of the world's most dangerous sharks.

Shark dive operators believe their businesses are part and parcel of shark conservation efforts. Enterprises like Shark Diving Unlimited, owned by South African Mike Rutzen, help drive the local economy while offering people a chance to behold the majesty of sharks up close. Each dive is an opportunity to teach the public about the creatures, and viewing them from the cage means that no shark will be harmed during the experience. Rutzen believes his business has created a demand for healthy, living sharks, rather than for their meat or body parts, as has been their worth in the past. As Rutzen put it, "My business gives the great whites a value alive, whereas previously their only value was their fins and jaws."[1] Facilitating enjoyable and thrilling experiences in the natural world has been a main conservationist strategy for years, and indeed, the increased interest in seeing sharks up close has inspired efforts to ensure that they thrive. "All in all, the tourism industry's profound fascination with sharks can generally be construed as a positive thing for one of the oldest of the charismatic megafauna on Earth,"[2] notes Rick Gaffney of Hawaii's Recreational Fishing Alliance.

Not everyone agrees that shark tourism goes hand in hand with conservation, however. Divers, surfers, and fishers are among the loudest opponents of shark tourism, claiming that the industry puts human lives at risk, and in turn, sharks, too. Chumming for sharks might alter the animals' natural feeding cycles and brings their population close to swimmers and beaches, which some claim increases the risk of an attack. In turn, shark attacks inflame antishark sentiments, which makes them more prone to hunting and decreases sympathy for conservation efforts.

South African water sports promoter Paul Botha is one person who argues that shark diving encourages sharks to attack humans, which in turn threatens their own populations. "The industry as a whole is conditioning the sharks; they are becoming bolder," warns Botha. "Parents in particular, whose children spend a lot of time in the water, feel very strongly about the shark cage diving and the conditioning of the sharks."[3] Botha charges that baiting the waters with chum is highly unethical and exploitative—a cheap way to ensure tourists get the thrill they paid for. "You don't chum for whales or put a dead mule at the waterhole when you're looking for lions," he argues. "If you want to see great whites, then get in a boat and go and look for them,"[4] he advises. Although the World Wildlife Federation and the Shark Trust, two prominent conservation organizations, have not found any compelling scientific evidence that links shark attacks with the increase in cage diving, opponents of the practice charge that shark tourist operations hide behind the front of conservation, when really they are just out to make a profit at the expense of both shark and human lives.

Shark tourism is one of many complex ocean-related issues that tiptoe along the line between conservationism and commercialism, a topic underlying many of the debates in the following chapters of

Introducing Issues with Opposing Viewpoints: Oceans. Students will consider arguments about whether and to what extent the ocean is changing, how various ocean species are coping with such changes, and what can and should be done to protect ocean habitats and ocean-dwelling animals. Carefully crafted guided reading questions and thought-provoking essays encourage students to develop their own opinions on these issues.

Notes

1. Quoted in Alex Duval Smith, "Is the Great White Shark in Danger?," *Guardian* (Manchester, UK), February 18, 2010. www.guardian .co.uk/travel/2010/feb/18/are-great-white-sharks-endangered.
2. Rick Gaffney, "Tourism and Jaws," Pacific Fisheries Coalition, 2000. www.pacfish.org/sharkcon/documents/gaffneyr.html.
3. Quoted in Liane Katz, "The Fin Edge of the Wedge?," *Guardian* (Manchester, UK), October 13, 2006. www.guardian.co.uk/trav el/2006/oct/13/adventure.extremesportsholidays.watersports holidays.
4. Quoted in Liane Katz, "The Fin Edge of the Wedge?"

Chapter 1

How Are Oceans Changing?

A Greenland glacier reaches the sea. Greenland's glaciers are melting twice as fast as they were ten years ago.

Oceans Are Warming

Mary Ann Whitley

"July [2009] was the hottest the world's oceans have been in almost 130 years of record-keeping."

The temperatures of the world's oceans are rising at an alarming rate, argues Mary Ann Whitley in the following viewpoint. She reports that ocean water in several places around the world—from Maine to the Arctic to the Gulf of Mexico—is significantly warmer than it has been in decades. Warmer ocean water is dangerous for the world's coral reefs and also threatens to melt glaciers and icebergs. It also contributes to increasingly frequent and violent hurricanes, contends Whitley. She concludes that the fact that oceans appear to be warming is a sure sign—and a worrisome one—of climate change. Whitley is a reporter for the *Plain Dealer,* a daily newspaper in Cleveland, Ohio.

AS YOU READ, CONSIDER THE FOLLOWING QUESTIONS:

1. How many degrees above average are temperatures in the Arctic, according to Whitley?
2. Why are warm ocean temperatures of more concern than warm temperatures on land, according to the author?
3. What effect does Whitley say warmer ocean temperatures have on coral reefs?

WASHINGTON—Steve Kramer spent an hour and a half swimming in the ocean Sunday—in Maine.

The water temperature was 72 degrees—more like Ocean City, Md., this time of year. And Ocean City's water temp hit 88 degrees this week, toasty even by Miami Beach standards.

Kramer, 26, who lives in the seaside town of Scarborough, said it was the first time he's ever swam so long in Maine's coastal waters. "Usually, you're in five minutes and you're out," he said.

It's not just the ocean off the Northeast coast that is super-warm this summer. July was the hottest the world's oceans have been in almost 130 years of record-keeping.

The average water temperature worldwide was 62.6 degrees, according to the National Climatic Data Center, the branch of the U.S. government that keeps world weather records. That was 1.1 degree higher than the 20th century average, and beat the previous high set in 1998 by a couple hundredths of a degree. The coolest recorded ocean temperature was 59.3 degrees in December 1909.

FAST FACT

According to the National Oceanic and Atmospheric Administration, the average global ocean surface temperature for June 2009 reached 62.6°F, the highest since record keeping for ocean temperatures began in 1880.

Meteorologists said there's a combination of forces at work this year: A natural El Nino system just getting started on top of worsening man-made global warming, and a dash of random weather variations. The resulting ocean heat is already harming threatened coral reefs. It could also hasten the melting of Arctic sea ice and help hurricanes strengthen.

The Gulf of Mexico, where warm water fuels hurricanes, has temperatures dancing around 90. Most of the water in the Northern Hemisphere has been considerably warmer than normal. The Mediterranean is about three degrees warmer than normal. Higher temperatures rule in the Pacific and Indian Oceans.

The heat is most noticeable near the Arctic, where water temperatures are as much as 10 degrees above average. The tongues of warm

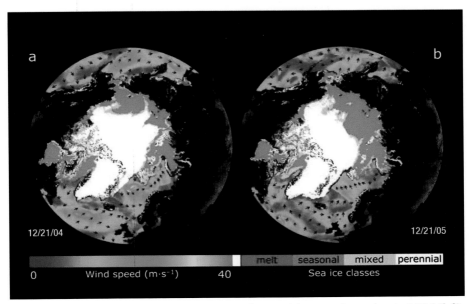

a

b

12/21/04

12/21/05

melt seasonal mixed perennial

0   Wind speed (m·s⁻¹)   40   Sea ice classes

These images from the National Aeronautics and Space Adminstration, taken in 2004 (left) and 2005, show the reduction of perennial ice (white) in the Arctic.

water could help melt sea ice from below and even cause thawing of ice sheets on Greenland, said Waleed Abdalati, director of the Earth Science and Observation Center at the University of Colorado.

Breaking heat records in water is more ominous as a sign of global warming than breaking temperature marks on land, because water takes longer to heat up and does not cool off as easily as land.

"This warm water we're seeing doesn't just disappear next year; it'll be around for a long time," said climate scientist Andrew Weaver of the University of Victoria in British Columbia. It takes five times more energy to warm water than land.

The warmer water "affects weather on the land," Weaver said. "This is another yet really important indicator of the change that's occurring."

Georgia Institute of Technology atmospheric science professor Judith Curry said water is warming in more places than usual, something that has not been seen in more than 50 years.

Add to that an unusual weather pattern this summer where the warmest temperatures seem to be just over oceans, while slightly cooler air is concentrated over land, said Deke Arndt, head of climate monitoring at the climate data center.

Global and Continental Temperature Change

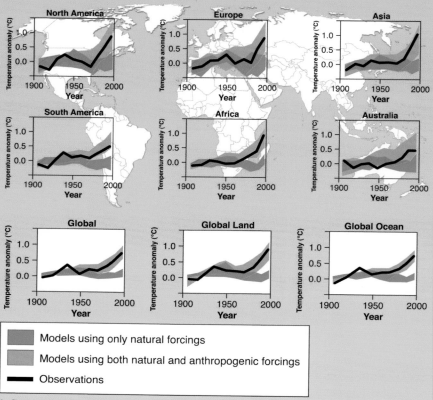

Taken from: Intergovernmental Panel on Climate Change, *Climate Change 2007: The Physical Science Basis, Summary for Policy Makers*, 2007, p. 11.

Influences exerted on a habitat or environment by nature are called natural forcings, while those exerted by humans are called anthropogenic forcings. Data and models from the Intergovernmental Panel on Climate Change show that temperatures have increased on every continent and in the world's oceans.

The pattern is so unusual that he suggested meteorologists may want to study that pattern to see what's behind it.

The effects of that warm water are already being seen in coral reefs, said C. Mark Eakin, coordinator of the National Oceanic and Atmospheric Administration's coral reef watch. Long-term excessive heat bleaches colorful coral reefs white and sometimes kills them.

Bleaching has started to crop up in the Florida Keys, Puerto Rico and the Virgin Islands—much earlier than usual. Typically, bleaching occurs after weeks or months of prolonged high water temperatures. That usually means September or October in the Caribbean, said Eakin. He found bleaching in Guam Wednesday. It's too early to know if the coral will recover or die. Experts are "bracing for another bad year," he said.

The problems caused by the El Nino pattern are likely to get worse, the scientists say.

An El Nino occurs when part of the central Pacific warms up, which in turn changes weather patterns worldwide for many months. El Nino and its cooling flip side, La Nina, happen every few years.

During an El Nino, temperatures on water and land tend to rise in many places, leading to an increase in the overall global average temperature. An El Nino has other effects, too, including dampening Atlantic hurricane formation and increasing rainfall and mudslides in Southern California.

Warm water is a required fuel for hurricanes. What's happening in the oceans "will add extra juice to the hurricanes," Curry said.

Hurricane activity has been quiet for much of the summer, but that may change soon, she said. Hurricane Bill quickly became a major storm and the National Hurricane Center warned that warm waters are along the path of the hurricane for the next few days.

Hurricanes need specific air conditions, so warmer water alone does not necessarily mean more or bigger storms, said James Franklin, chief hurricane specialist at the National Hurricane Center in Miami.

EVALUATING THE AUTHORS' ARGUMENTS:

In this viewpoint Mary Ann Whitley says that ocean temperatures are the warmest on record in more than a century. In the following viewpoint Lorne Gunter says that a rise in ocean temperatures has not been detected. How might you account for the stark differences in the opinions of these two authors? Explain your reasoning and quote from both texts in your answer.

Oceans Are Cooling

Lorne Gunter

"*In five years, the [buoys] have failed to detect any global warming. They are not reinforcing the scientific orthodoxy of the day; namely that man is causing the planet to warm dangerously.*"

In the following viewpoint Lorne Gunter argues that global ocean temperatures are not rising; rather, they are cooling. Gunter explains that high-tech buoys that measure ocean temperature very accurately have not revealed any warming trend—in fact, they have detected a slight decline in temperature. Gunter explains that there are scientists and politicians who want to believe so badly in global warming that they are willing to deny, ignore, or otherwise brush aside this evidence. In Gunter's opinion, the fact that oceans are not warming is proof that climate change models are probably wrong. He thinks the world is not experiencing a dangerous warming trend and concludes people who push such a view are alarmist.

Gunter is a Canadian journalist who works at the *Edmonton Journal*, in the province of Alberta, where he has published more than thirteen hundred columns. His essays have also appeared in the *Globe and Mail* (Toronto) and in *Readers' Digest*, *National Review*, and the *Weekly Standard* in the United States.

AS YOU READ, CONSIDER THE FOLLOWING QUESTIONS:
  1. What are Argo buoys, as described by the author? How do they work?
  2. What does the word *dogma* mean in the context of the viewpoint?
  3. What have NASA's eight weather satellites revealed about global warming over the past thirty years, according to Gunter?

They drift along in the worlds' oceans at a depth of 2,000 metres—more than a mile deep—constantly monitoring the temperature, salinity, pressure and velocity of the upper oceans. Then, about once every 10 days, a bladder on the outside of these buoys inflates and raises them slowly to the surface, gathering data about each strata of seawater they pass through. After an upward journey of nearly six hours, the Argo monitors bob on the waves while an onboard transmitter sends their information to a satellite that in turn retransmits it to several land-based research computers where it may be accessed by anyone who wishes to see it.

No Evidence of Warming

These 3,000 yellow sentinels—about the size and shape of a large fence post—free-float the world's oceans, season in and season out, surfacing between 30 and 40 times a year, disgorging their findings, then submerging again for another fact-finding voyage.

It's fascinating to watch their progress online. (The URLs are too complex to reproduce here, but Google "Argo Buoy Movement" or "Argo Float Animation," and you will be directed to the links.)

When they were first deployed in 2003, the Argos were hailed for their ability to collect information on ocean conditions more precisely, at more places and greater depths and in more conditions than ever before. No longer would scientists have to rely on measurements mostly at the surface from older scientific buoys or inconsistent shipboard monitors.

So why are some scientists now beginning to question the buoys' findings? Because in five years, the little blighters have failed to detect any global warming. They are not reinforcing the scientific orthodoxy of the day; namely that man is causing the planet to warm danger-ously. They are not proving the predetermined conclusions of their human masters. Therefore they, and not their masters' hypotheses, must be wrong.

In fact, "there has been a very slight cooling," according to a U.S. National Public Radio (NPR) interview with Josh Willis at NASA's [National Aeronautics and Space Administration's] Jet Propulsion Laboratory, a scientist who keeps close watch on the Argo findings.

Clinging to the Theory of Warming

Dr. Willis insisted the temperature drop was "not anything really significant." And I trust he's right. But can anyone imagine NASA or the National Oceanic and Atmospheric Administration (NOAA) or the Intergovernmental Panel on Climate Change—the UN's climate experts—shrugging off even a "very slight" warming?

A slight drop in the oceans' temperature over a period of five or six years probably is insignificant, just as a warming over such a short

Scientists use probes like this one to provide data on ocean conditions and temperatures.

period would be. Yet if there had been a rise of any kind, even of the same slightness, rest assured this would be broadcast far and wide as yet another log on the global warming fire.

Just look how tenaciously some scientists are prepared to cling to the climate change dogma. "It may be that we are in a period of less rapid warming," Dr. Willis told NPR.

Yeah, you know, like when you put your car into reverse you are causing it to enter a period of less rapid forward motion. Or when I gain a few pounds I am in a period of less rapid weight loss.

Climate Change Models May Be Wrong

The big problem with the Argo findings is that all the major climate computer models [used by scientists to predict changes to different regions of the world based on increasing levels of carbon dioxide] postulate that as much as 80–90% of global warming will result from the oceans warming rapidly then releasing their heat into the atmosphere.

But if the oceans aren't warming, then (please whisper) perhaps the models are wrong.

The supercomputer models also can't explain the interaction of clouds and climate. They have no idea whether clouds warm the world more by trapping heat in or cool it by reflecting heat back into space.

Modellers are also perplexed by the findings of NASA's eight weather satellites that take more than 300,000 temperature readings daily over the entire surface of the Earth, versus approximately 7,000 random readings from Earth stations.

In nearly 30 years of operation, the satellites have discovered a warming trend of just 0.14 [degrees] C per decade, less than the models and well within the natural range of temperature variation.

I'm not saying for sure the models are wrong and the Argos and satellites are right, only that in a debate as critical as the one on climate, it would be nice to hear some alternatives to the alarmist theory.

EVALUATING THE AUTHOR'S ARGUMENTS:

To make his point Lorne Gunter characterizes weight gain as "less rapid weight loss" and driving in reverse as "less rapid forward motion." What does he mean by this? What does it have to do with climate change and whether the oceans are warming? After explaining what the author means, state whether or not you agree with him.

Ocean Levels Are Rising

Rob Young and Orrin Pilkey

"Certainly, no one should be expecting less than a three-foot rise in sea level this century."

In the following viewpoint Rob Young and Orrin Pilkey warn that the rise in ocean levels will be much greater than current models predict. They explain that reports from the Intergovernmental Panel on Climate Change (IPCC) have failed to calculate sea level rise accurately and have thus dramatically understated the problem. Rather than the two-foot rise predicted by the IPCC, the authors predict that by 2100, sea levels will have risen by at least seven feet, possibly more. Rising sea levels threaten crops, property, and even the land masses of entire cities and nations. The authors conclude that governments must act immediately to protect their citizens from the impending catastrophic rise in ocean levels.

Young is the director of the Program for the Study of Developed Shorelines at Western Carolina University. Pilkey is a professor emeritus in Duke University's Division of Earth and Ocean Science. They coauthored *The Rising Sea*, published by Island Press.

AS YOU READ, CONSIDER THE FOLLOWING QUESTIONS:
1. How many people do the authors say will become refugees when the nation of Bangladesh is flooded with seawater?
2. By how many feet do Young and Pilkey warn that sea levels will rise if the entire West Antarctic Ice Sheet melts?
3. List at least five US cities the authors say are most threatened by rising sea levels.

T he reports from the Intergovernmental Panel on Climate Change (IPCC) are balanced and comprehensive documents summarizing the impact of global warming on the planet. But they are not without imperfections, and one of the most notable was the analysis of future sea level rise contained in the latest report, issued in 2007.

A Critical Report Got It Wrong

Given the complexities of forecasting how much the melting of the Greenland and West Antarctic ice sheets [a mass of glacial land ice extending more than 20,000 square miles] will contribute to increases in global sea level, the IPCC chose not to include these giant ice masses in their calculations, thus ignoring what is likely to be the most important source of sea level rise in the 21st century. Arguing that too little was understood about ice sheet collapse to construct a mathematical model upon which even a rough estimate could be based, the IPCC came up with sea level predictions using thermal expansion of the oceans and melting of mountain glaciers outside the poles. Its results were predictably conservative— a maximum of a two-foot rise this century—and were even a foot lower than an earlier IPCC report that factored in some melting of Greenland's ice sheet.

The IPCC's 2007 sea level calculations—widely recognized by the academic community as a critical flaw in the report—have caused confusion among many in the general public and the media and have created fodder for global warming skeptics. But there should be no confusion about the serious threat posed by rising sea levels, especially as evidence has mounted in the past two years [2008 to

2010] of the accelerated pace of melting of the Greenland and West Antarctic ice sheets.

The Seas Will Rise Dramatically

The message for the world's leaders and decision makers is that sea level rise is real and is only going to get worse. Indeed, we make the case in our recent book, *The Rising Sea*, that governments and coastal managers should assume the inevitability of a seven-foot rise in sea level. This number is not a prediction. But we believe that seven feet is the most prudent, conservative long-term planning guideline for coastal cities and communities, especially for the siting of major infrastructure; a number of academic studies examining recent ice sheet dynamics have suggested that an increase of seven feet or more is not only possible, but likely. Certainly, no one should be expecting less than a three-foot rise in sea level this century.

Scientists from the Intergovernmental Panel on Climate Change (IPCC) testify before the House Science and Technology Committee on Climate Change. The IPCC has been criticized for not including in their reports data from melting Greenland and West Antarctic Ice Sheets.

In the 20th century, sea level rise was primarily due to thermal expansion of ocean water. Contributions of melting mountain glaciers and the large ice sheets were minor components. But most climate scientists now believe that the main drivers of sea level rise in the 21st century will be the melting of the West Antarctic Ice Sheet (a potential of a 16-foot rise if the entire sheet melts) and the Greenland Ice Sheet (a potential rise of 20 feet if the entire ice cap melts). The nature of the melting is non-linear and is difficult to predict.

A Rise of Three, Four, Even Seven Feet

Seeking to correct the IPCC's failure to come up with a comprehensive forecast for sea level increase, a number of state panels and government committees have produced sea level rise predictions that include an examination of melting ice sheets. For example, sea level rise panels in Rhode Island and [Florida's] Miami-Dade County have concluded that a minimum of a three- to five-foot sea level rise should be anticipated by 2100. A California report assumes a possible 4.6-foot rise by 2100, while the Dutch assume a 2.5-foot rise by 2050 in the design of their tidal gates.

Given the growing consensus about the major sea level rise on the way in the coming century or two, the continued development of many low-lying coastal areas—including much of the U.S. east coast—is foolhardy and irresponsible.

Chaos and Instability Will Result

Rising seas will be on the front lines of the battle against changing climate during the next century. Our great concern is that as the infrastructure of major cities in the industrialized world becomes threatened, there will be few resources left to address the dramatic impacts that will be facing the citizens of the developing world.

The ramifications of a major sea level rise are massive. Agriculture will be disrupted, water supplies will be salinized, storms and flood waters will reach ever further inland, and millions of environmental refugees will be created—15 million people live at or below three feet elevation in Bangladesh, for example. Governments, especially

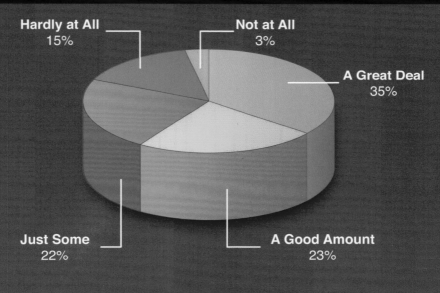

Americans Worry About Rising Sea Levels

An ABC News/*Washington Post*/Stanford University poll found the majority of Americans are concerned about a rise in sea level due to global warming. Fifty-eight percent of Americans are concerned either "a great deal" or "a good amount" about rising seas.

Question:
"How much does a rise in sea level due to global warming concern you: a great deal, a good amount, just some, or hardly at all?"

Hardly at All
15%

Not at All
3%

A Great Deal
35%

Just Some
22%

A Good Amount
23%

Taken from: ABC News/*Washington Post*/Stanford University poll, April 5–10, 2007.

those in the developing world, will be disrupted, creating political instability.

The most vulnerable of all coastal environments are deltas of major rivers, including the Mekong [in Vietnam], Irrawaddy [in Myanmar], Niger [in Nigeria], Ganges-Brahmaputra [in India and Bangladesh], Nile [Egypt], and Mississippi [United States]. Here, land subsidence will combine with global sea level rise to create very high rates of what is known as "local, relative sea level rise." The rising seas will displace the vast majority of people in these delta regions. Adding insult to injury, in many parts of Asia the rice crop will be decimated by rising sea level—a three-foot sea level rise will eliminate half of the rice production in Vietnam—causing a food crisis coincident with the mass migration of people.

Devastating Changes Already Underway

The Mississippi Delta is unique because it lies within a country with the financial resources to fight land loss. Nevertheless, we believe multibillion-dollar engineering and restoration efforts designed to preserve communities on the Mississippi Delta are doomed to failure, given the magnitude of relative sea level rise expected. Former Secretary of the Interior Bruce Babbitt said in 2008 that it was an "ineluctable [undeniable] fact" that within the lifespan of some people alive today, "the vast majority of that land will be underwater." He also faulted federal officials for not developing migration plans for area residents and for not having the "honesty and compassion" to tell Louisiana residents the "truth": Someday, they will have to leave the delta. The city of New Orleans can probably be protected into the next century, but only at great expense and with little guarantee that future storms like Hurricane Katrina will not inundate the city again.

FAST FACT

The Intergovernmental Panel on Climate Change predicts that ocean levels will rise by between 7.5 inches and 17 inches by 2100.

Pacific and Indian Ocean atoll [a group of closely spaced coral islands circling or nearly circling a shallow lagoon] nations are already being abandoned because of the direct and indirect effects of sea level rise, such as saltwater intrusion into groundwater. In the Marshall Islands, some crops are being grown in abandoned 55-gallon oil drums because the ground is now too salty for planting. New Zealand is accepting, on a gradual basis, all of the inhabitants of the Tuvalu atolls. Inhabitants of Carteret Atoll have all moved to Papua, New Guinea. The forward-looking government of the Maldives recently held a cabinet meeting underwater to highlight the ultimate fate of their small island nation.

The world's major coastal cities will undoubtedly receive most of the attention as sea level rise threatens infrastructure. Miami tops the

Changes in Temperature, Sea Level, and Northern Hemisphere Snow Cover

Data from the Intergovernmental Panel on Climate Change show that since 1850, temperatures have increased, snow cover has melted, and sea levels have risen.

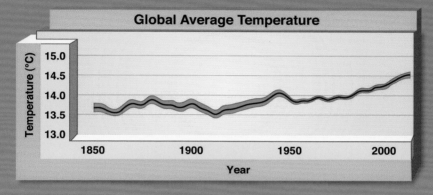

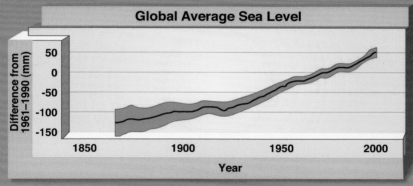

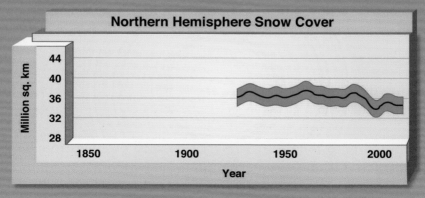

Taken from: Intergovernmental Panel on Climate Change, *Climate Change 2007: The Physical Science Basis, Summary for Policymakers*, 2007, p. 6.

list of most endangered cities in the world, as measured by the value of property that would be threatened by a three-foot rise. This would flood all of Miami Beach and leave downtown Miami sitting as an island of water, disconnected from the rest of Florida. Other threatened U.S. cities include New York/Newark, New Orleans, Boston, Washington, Philadelphia, Tampa-St. Petersburg, and San Francisco. Osaka/Kobe, Tokyo [Japan], Rotterdam, Amsterdam [Netherlands], and Nagoya [Japan] are among the most threatened major cities outside of North America.

Preserving coastal cities will require huge public expenditures, leaving smaller coastal resort communities to fend for themselves. Manhattan, for example, is likely to beat out Nags Head, North Carolina for federal funds, a fact that recreational beach communities must recognize when planning a response to sea level rise.

Our Leaders Must Act

Twelve percent of the world's open ocean shorelines are fronted by barrier islands, and a three-foot sea level rise will spell doom for development on most of them—save for those completely surrounded by massive seawalls. Impacts in the United States, with a 3,500-mile-long barrier island shoreline extending from Montauk Point on Long Island to the Mexican border, will be huge. The only way to preserve the barrier islands themselves will be to abandon them so that they may respond naturally to rising sea level. Yet, most coastal states continue to allow massive, irresponsible development of the low-lying coast.

Ironically, low-elevation Florida is probably the least prepared of all coastal states. Hundreds of miles of high rises line the state's shoreline, and more are built every year. The state pours subsidies into coastal development through state-run insurance and funding for coastal protection. If a portion of those funds were spent adapting to sea level rise rather than ignoring it, Florida might be ready to meet the challenge of the next century. Let's hope the state rises to the challenge. . . .

Responding to long-term sea level rise will pose unprecedented challenges to the international community. Economic and humanitarian disasters can be avoided, but only through wise, forward-looking planning. Tough decisions will need to be made regarding the allocation of resources and response to natural disasters. Let us hope that our political leadership can provide the bold vision and strong leadership that will be required to implement a reasoned response.

EVALUATING THE AUTHORS' ARGUMENTS:

Rob Young and Orrin Pilkey are scientists who specialize in the area of ocean science and coastal development. Does knowing their background make you more likely to agree with them that ocean levels are rising? If so, why? If not, why not? Explain to what extent you think a person's credentials affect his or her credibility when it comes to making persuasive arguments.

Viewpoint 4

Ocean Levels Are Not Rising

Marc Sheppard

> "*Narrowly isolated melting doesn't support the hypothesis of widespread polar warming necessary to kindle such horrific images of metropolises submerged by anthropogenic impropriety.*"

Ocean levels are not dangerously rising, nor is there any reason to think they will, argues Marc Sheppard in the following viewpoint. He claims that believers in global warming look very narrowly at evidence when they claim the seas are rising—they look only at small areas of polar regions, and fail to take into account the area in its totality, he maintains. If they did, he argues, they would see that most of Antarctica has cooled in recent decades and that most of the water underneath it has remained nearly frozen in the last five years. Sheppard says that no catastrophic or devastating melting is taking place, and thus rises in ocean level will probably remain modest and consistent in the coming centuries. He concludes that global warming proponents should stop pushing a doomsday scenario that envisions the world's cities drowning as the result of catastrophic sea rise.

Sheppard is the environment editor of *American Thinker*, a daily online journal.

AS YOU READ, CONSIDER THE FOLLOWING QUESTIONS:
1. Who is Ole Anders Nøst and how does he factor into the author's argument?
2. Approximately how many inches per century have sea levels risen since the Little Ice Age ended, according to Sheppard?
3. What, according to the author, has remained virtually unchanged since it was first measured in 1979?

On Monday [January 12, 2010], scientists from the Norwegian Polar Institute [NPI] reported that they'd measured sea temperatures beneath an East Antarctic ice shelf [a permanent floating sheet of ice attached to a landmass] and found no signs of warming whatsoever. And while the discovery's corollaries remain mostly blurred by the few rogue mainstream media outlets actually reporting it, the findings are in fact yet another serious blow to the sky-is-falling-because-oceans-are-rising prophecies of the climate alarm crowd.

Looking Too Narrowly at the Evidence

For years now, alarmists have insisted that Antarctica is thawing thanks to man-made global warming. They warn that such melting of a frozen continent containing 90 percent of all the ice on the planet would inevitably lead to a cataclysmic sea level rise (SLR). Scary stuff, indeed.

However, there are several problems with their assertions, not the least of which is that all evidence of melting selectively focuses on the only area of the continent satellite evidence confirms is warming—the western region in general, and the Antarctic Peninsula in particular.

But as ICECAP's [International Climate and Environmental Change Assessment Project's] Joe D'Aleo observed in 2008, the relatively small area of the peninsula offers an extremely poor representative sample, as it juts out well north of the mainland into an area of the South Atlantic well known for its "surface and subsurface active volcanic activity." And in the greater scheme, adds D'Aleo, "the vast continent has actually cooled since 1979."

Still, carbo-chondriacs blame the "collapse" of ten ice shelves in and around the peninsula on melting of the underside of the ice by global-warming-fueled rising ocean temperatures. And they insist that their

Aerial photographs show the effects of melting ice on Antarctica's western peninsula. Overall temperatures on the Antarctic continent have risen since 1979.

models are spot-on in predicting that unless mankind stops pumping CO_2 into the atmosphere, it's only a matter of time before the entire continent melts. The effect of such an event, they caution, would be nothing short of a civilization-ending, 57-meter SLR—a vision normally reserved to biblical fables or the wild imagination of [former vice president and environmentalist] Al Gore.

Of course, narrowly isolated melting doesn't support the hypothesis of widespread polar warming necessary to kindle such horrific images of metropolises submerged by anthropogenic impropriety. That's why locating and denouncing diminishing ice east of the Transantarctic Mountains ranks high on every green-funded researcher's to-do list. And that's also why it would appear that NPI scientists thought they had hit the jackpot when their models calculated that the ice shelves at Dronning Maud Land along Antarctica's northeastern border should be melting at the same rate as those farther west.

No Signs of Increased Melting

So last November [2009], a team from NPI set out to investigate the status of just such a locale—the Fimbul Ice Shelf. Their stated primary mission: to determine whether ice masses on the shelf are indeed currently on the decline.

Last month [December 2009], the expedition drilled its first borehole into the 250-to-400-meter-thick floating ice in order to study the melting and ocean circulation underneath. But readings revealed by the instruments they lowered into the water below were not quite what was anticipated.

In fact, contrary to the warmer, ice-melting temperatures predicted by models, NPI oceanographer and project leader Ole Anders Nøst reported that "the water under the ice shelf is very close to the freezing point." Furthermore, there seemed to have been no change in almost five years:

> We observed a roughly 50 meter deep layer of water with temperatures very close to the freezing point, about -2.05 degree [Celsius], just beneath the ice shelf. The highest observed temperature was about -1.83 degrees close to the bottom. The temperatures are very similar to temperature data collected by [equipment attached to] elephant seals in 2008 and by British Antarctic Survey using an autosub below the ice shelf in 2005.

Nøst concluded that "This situation seems to be stable, suggesting that the melting under the ice shelf does not increase."

Sea Level Rise Remains Steady

As to the ocean circulation models that incorrectly showed "warm deep water flowing in under the ice shelves," Nøst admitted that "as this is not observed, the models are most likely wrong and should be improved."

Translation: In contrast to model forecasts, Antarctic ice shelf collapse still appears to be isolated to a very tiny area in the western region of a continent otherwise experiencing continued glacial and ice shelf advancement.

And that fact certainly casts further serious doubt on the U.N.'s most recent century-end SLR predictions. Last year, the 18- to 59-centimeter estimate that appeared in the Intergovernmental Panel on Climate Change (IPCC) 2007 Fourth Assessment Report (AR4) was increased to a full two meters, *based entirely on fears of accelerated glacial melting in Greenland and Antarctica*. Keep in mind that since the prolonged cold snap of the Little Ice Age ended in 1850, the global rate of SLR has remained essentially steady at approximately seven inches per century, due largely to thermal expansion.

Reality check time: Does anything [about this] suggest to you that SLR might increase over *tenfold*—as the IPCC now predicts—this century?

Severe Melting Will Take Thousands of Years

As such, is it any wonder that alarmists now claim that even a few degrees of warming will ignite enough accelerated liquefying of the petatons of Earth's surface ice to render the planet barely inhabitable by land-dwellers?

In fact, it was just months after the release of AR4 that the Union of Concerned Scientists [UCS] offered these hyperactive projections to the 2007 U.N. Framework Convention on Climate Change in Bali: Sustained warming of [2°C above pre-industrial levels] could, for example, result in the extinction of many species and extensive melting of the Greenland and West Antarctic ice sheets [WAIS]—causing global sea level to rise between 12 and 40 feet.

Readers should be aware that the WAIS [that] UCS referred to are not to be confused with aforementioned ice shelves. While melting "sheets," which predominately lie above bedrock, might contribute to SLR, the ice "shelves" float atop the water and therefore have ostensibly the same impact on SLR frozen as they would melted. There has, however, been concern expressed that melting glaciers might flow faster toward the ocean if unencumbered by the barricading effect of the shelves.

Now, even the notoriously alarmist U.K. Met Office admits that the complete Greenland meltdown to which they'd attribute a seven-meter SLR "would take thousands of years" even if temperatures were to continue to climb. It's therefore quite logical to assume that the majority of the predicted SLR is expected to originate in Antarctica.

Antarctica Is Not Melting at All

And yet, other than select ice shelves (which again are already afloat and would have no further impact upon SLR) in one minuscule area soaking in water warmed by volcanic activity, Antarctica isn't melting at all. And with air temperatures averaging consistently below zero and water temperatures barely above freezing—even in summer—nothing in the foreseeable future suggests it might—not even should temperatures, which have been falling since 1998, nonetheless rise to the mostly arbitrary yet internationally alarmist-approved catastrophic level of 2°C above pre-industrial levels.

In fact, despite the IPCC insistence that global warming will be most prevalent at the poles, southern-hemisphere sea ice area has remained virtually unchanged since satellite sensors and analytical programs were first capable of measuring it in 1979.

So perhaps when the green-gospel-pronouncing IPCC releases its Fifth Assessment Report, tentatively due for 2014, contributors and lead authors alike might carefully consider the NPI findings, the steady rate of SLR over the past 150 years, and the overall resilience of Antarctic ice before formulating their next soggy doom-and-gloom prophecy. (And don't forget this undeniable fact: Across the continent, the 2008–2009 southern hemisphere summer hosted the lowest Antarctic ice melt in thirty years.)

Surely were these people bound by scientific concerns exclusively, there'd be no doubt whatsoever that they'd do just that.

EVALUATING THE AUTHORS' ARGUMENTS:

The author of this viewpoint, Marc Sheppard, and the authors of the previous viewpoint, Rob Young and Orrin Pilkey, discuss the West Antarctic Ice Shelves and Ice Sheets but make very different statements and predictions about them. Sum up these authors' positions on the West Antarctic Ice Sheet and how these factor into their arguments.

Oceans Are Becoming Dangerously Acidic

Natural Resources Defense Council

"Researchers predict that if carbon emissions continue at their current rate, ocean acidity will more than double by 2100."

In the following viewpoint the Natural Resources Defense Council (NRDC) argues that the world's oceans are becoming dangerously acidic. The author explains that carbon dioxide—a by-product of man-made activities and a greenhouse gas believed to be causing global warming—is being absorbed by the world's oceans and making them increasingly acidic. The NRDC explains that ocean acidification threatens coral reefs and the staggering array of animals and humans that depend on them. Also threatened by acidification are small animals, which are a critical food source for larger animals. The NRDC warns that ocean acidification threatens not just marine life but the human activities that depend on healthy oceans.

With 1.3 million members and the help of more than 350 lawyers, scientists, and other professionals, the NRDC is among the most powerful environmental activist organizations in the United States.

AS YOU READ, CONSIDER THE FOLLOWING QUESTIONS:
1. How many billion tons of CO_2 does the author say the oceans have absorbed in the last 250 years?
2. What does the NRDC warn might happen to the Southern Ocean around Antarctica by 2050?
3. What are pteropods and coccolithophores, and how do they factor into the author's argument?

E arth's atmosphere isn't the only victim of burning fossil fuels. About a quarter of all carbon dioxide emissions are absorbed by the earth's oceans, where they're having an impact that's just starting to be understood.

Over the last decade, scientists have discovered that this excess CO_2 is actually changing the chemistry of the sea and proving harmful for many forms of marine life. This process is known as ocean acidification.

A more acidic ocean could wipe out species, disrupt the food web and impact fishing, tourism and any other human endeavor that relies on the sea.

The change is happening fast—and it will take fast action to slow or stop it. Over the last 250 years, oceans have absorbed 530 billion tons of CO_2, triggering a 30 percent increase in ocean acidity.

FAST FACT

Based on current rates of CO_2 emissions, by the end of the twenty-first century global ocean acidity will increase by 150 percent, according to a report published in the journal *Nature*.

Before people started burning coal and oil, ocean pH [a measure of acidity] had been relatively stable for the previous 20 million years. But researchers predict that if carbon emissions continue at their current rate, ocean acidity will more than double by 2100.

The polar regions will be the first to experience changes. Projections show that the Southern Ocean around Antarctica will actually become corrosive by 2050.

Corrosive Impacts on Sea Life

The new chemical composition of our oceans is expected to harm a wide range of ocean life—particularly creatures with shells. The resulting disruption to the ocean ecosystem could have a widespread ripple effect and further deplete already struggling fisheries worldwide.

The Changing pH of the Ocean

pH is a measure of acidity. The pH of ocean water has always been about 8.16, but in recent years it has fallen to 8.05 and may fall another 0.4 units by 2100. Some say this increasing acidification threatens marine life.

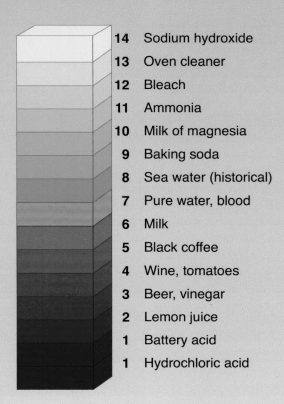

14	Sodium hydroxide
13	Oven cleaner
12	Bleach
11	Ammonia
10	Milk of magnesia
9	Baking soda
8	Sea water (historical)
7	Pure water, blood
6	Milk
5	Black coffee
4	Wine, tomatoes
3	Beer, vinegar
2	Lemon juice
1	Battery acid
1	Hydrochloric acid

Taken from: Richard A. Feely et al. "Carbon Dioxide and Our Ocean Legacy," Pew Trust; Center for Ocean Solutions, 2006.

OCEAN ACIDIFICATION

Climate change is turning the oceans more acid in a trend that could threaten fisheries production and is already causing the fastest shift in ocean chemistry in 65 million years, a U.N. study showed on Thursday

COP16
CMP6 México2010

HOW ACIDIFICATION OCCURS

Absorbing carbon dioxide triggers chemical reactions which can make oceans more acidic. The world's oceans currently soak up about 11 billion tonnes of carbon dioxide each year

1 Carbon dioxide absorbed from the air combines with water to form carbonic acid

2 Increased levels of carbonic acid lowers the ocean's pH level, making it more acidic

3 Acidity decreases the concentration of carbonate, a compound vital the building of coral reefs

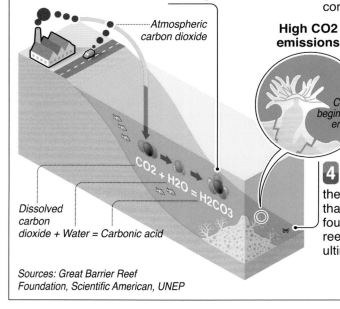

Atmospheric carbon dioxide

High CO2 emissions

Coral grows

Coral begins to erode

Reduced emissions

$CO_2 + H_2O = H_2CO_3$

Dissolved carbon dioxide + Water = Carbonic acid

4 Without carbonate, corals cannot build the skeletal structure that provides the foundation for coral reefs. The reef structure ultimately erodes away

Sources: Great Barrier Reef Foundation, Scientific American, UNEP

REUTERS

Increased acidity reduces carbonate—the mineral used to form the shells and skeletons of many shellfish and corals. The effect is similar to osteoporosis, slowing growth and making shells weaker. If pH levels drop enough, the shells will literally dissolve.

This process will not only harm some of our favorite seafood, such as lobster and mussels, but will also injure some species of smaller marine organisms—things such as pteropods and coccolithophores. You've probably never heard of them, but they form a vital part of the food web. If those smaller organisms are wiped out, the larger animals that feed on them could suffer as well.

Disappearing Coral Reefs
Delicate corals may face an even greater risk than shellfish because they require very high levels of carbonate to build their skeletons.

Acidity slows reef-building, which could lower the resiliency of corals and lead to their erosion and eventual extinction. The "tipping point" for coral reefs could happen as soon as 2050.

Coral reefs serve as the home for many other forms of ocean life. Their disappearance would be akin to rainforests being wiped out worldwide. Such losses would reverberate throughout the marine environment and have profound social impacts as well—especially on the fishing and tourism industries.

The loss of coral reefs would also reduce the protection that they offer coastal communities against storms surges and hurricanes—which might become more severe with warmer air and sea surface temperatures due to global warming.

What Can We Do About It?
Combating acidification requires reducing CO_2 emissions and improving the health of the oceans. Creating marine protected areas (essentially national parks for the sea) and stopping destructive fishing practices would increase the resiliency of marine ecosystems and help them withstand acidification.

Evidence suggests that coral reefs in protected ocean reserves are less affected by global threats such as global warming and ocean acidification, demonstrating the power of ecosystem protection.

Ultimately, though, reducing the amount of carbon dioxide absorbed into the oceans may be the only way to halt acidification. The same strategies needed to fight global warming on land can also help in the seas.

The acidification of our oceans is the hidden side of the world's carbon crisis, says Lisa Suatoni, an NRDC [National Resources Defenses Council] ocean scientist, and only reinforces that we need to make changes in how we fuel our world—and we need to do it quickly.

EVALUATING THE AUTHOR'S ARGUMENTS:

The Natural Resources Defense Council uses facts, statistics, examples, and persuasive reasoning to make its argument that the world's oceans are becoming dangerously acidic. It does not, however, use any quotations to support its points. If you were to rewrite this article and insert quotations, what authorities might you quote? Where would you place the quotations, and why?

The Threat of Ocean Acidification Is Exaggerated

Tim Ball

"The idea that a 0.1 pH unit increase [in ocean acidity] is significant is ludicrous."

The concept of ocean acidification is the latest in a long line of global warming scare scenarios, argues Tim Ball in the following viewpoint. He explains that ocean acidification—the theory that oceans absorb excess atmospheric carbon dioxide, turning it into an acidic compound that threatens marine life—is flawed in two ways. For one, Ball rejects claims that there is a threatening increase in atmospheric carbon dioxide that is causing climate change. Secondly, Ball says that even if the oceans were absorbing excess carbon dioxide, it would not cause significant or threatening changes. He concludes that the concept of ocean acidification has been dreamed up by global warming alarmists who feel compelled to scare others about what he says are normal and natural environmental changes. Ball is a former climatology professor at the University of Winnipeg in Canada. He has served as an adviser to the International Climate Science Coalition, Friends of Science, and the Frontier Centre for Public Policy.

AS YOU READ, CONSIDER THE FOLLOWING QUESTIONS:
1. Why does Ball think estimates and computer models are questionable ways of determining ocean acidification?
2. What does the author say are two requirements of scare scenarios, and how are these applied to the issue of ocean acidification?
3. What did Tom Tripp state, as quoted by Ball, in July 2009?

A s public awareness grows that human-caused warming is false the extent and degree of attempts to scare the public increases. The scare preference is for remote geographic areas such as the Arctic or Antarctic or complex obscure topics ideally with global implications, which the public knows little about. The latest scare story is ocean acidification, which combines these traits with the advantage of a word with negative connotations and used before in *acid rain*.

A Classic Scare Story

Like all scares it is based on total acceptance that an increase in atmospheric CO_2 is a problem. The claim in this case is it is causing temperature increase, but also changing the chemistry of the oceans. Like all the scares it is pure speculation after you accept the false claim [that] CO_2 is causing temperature increase. To counteract suggestions that they are overstating the threat they use a form of the precautionary principle, which holds [that] we must act anyway. So the problem exists, it is just a matter of the extent of the impact. Yet the full impact of ocean acidification and how these impacts may propagate through marine ecosystems and affect fisheries remains largely unknown.

Oceans absorb or release CO_2 primarily determined by the amount in the atmosphere and the water temperature. The argument is that regardless of what the air temperature does, increased CO_2 amounts in the atmosphere due to human activity guarantees more going into the oceans. This change results in a change in water chemistry reflected in one measure, the pH.

A solution has a pH level that is a measure of the acidity or alkalinity [of the solution]. The pH scale is from 0 to 14 and a measure of 7 is neutral. The scale is created relative to standard solutions and agreed on internationally. Above 7 the solution is more alkaline and below 7 it is more acid. The oceans are considered to have a pH of 8.2 with a variance of 0.3, so it is an alkaline solution.

Questionable Claims, Questionable Science

The claim of ocean acidification is based on estimates and computer models; these use the very questionable pre-industrial atmospheric level of CO_2 to calculate an increase of about 0.1 pH units. Of course, the Intergovernmental Panel on Climate Change (IPCC) attributes the CO_2 increase to human production, which is wrong because the global carbon cycle is very vague about sources, storage and length of time in each condition. For example, the error in the estimate of CO_2 from the oceans each year is greater than the total human contribution.

The idea that a 0.1 pH unit increase is significant is ludicrous when the estimate has a range of 0.3 units. There is a subtle but important point here because words are part of the scare component. Even if you accept the claimed change, it is not acidification; it is proper to say the solution is becoming less alkaline, but that doesn't sound threatening. More problematic is the validity of the measures. Although pH in seawater has been measured for many decades, a reliable long-term trend of ocean water pH cannot be established due to data quality issues, in particular the lack of strict and stable calibration procedures and standards. Moreover, seawater pH is very sensitive to temperature, and temperature is not always recorded or measured at sufficient accuracy to constrain the pH measurement.

> **FAST FACT**
>
> A 2009 study published in the journal *Estuarine, Coastal and Shelf Science* found that marine organisms show a variety of responses to elevated ocean acidity; some are far more resistant to ocean acidification than previously believed.

Even if CO_2 increases to 560 ppm [parts per million] by 2050, as the IPCC predict, it would only result in a 0.2 unit reduction of pH. This is still within the error of the estimate of global average.

French explorer Jean-Louis Etienne takes off in a hot air balloon to cross the Arctic from Norway to Alaska in April 2010. He monitored the level of CO_2 in the atmosphere at the North Pole.

The Real Threat Is Alarmism

So what is threatened by this reduced alkalinity? Most marine life if you read all the stories, but, scare stories need one issue [that] people view positively. Coral fits the bill well because the underwater scenes of color and diversity of life [in a reef] mesmerize us all. According to the experts, ocean acidification may render most regions of the ocean inhospitable to coral reefs by 2050, if atmospheric CO_2 levels continue to increase. It could lead to substantial changes in commercial fish stocks, threatening food security for millions of people as well as the multi-billion dollar fishing industry.

Scares require dramatic change beyond any previously recorded. For instance: "Ocean acidification is more rapid than ever in the history of the earth and if you look at the pCO_2 (partial pressure of carbon dioxide) levels we have reached now, you have to go back 35 million years in time to find the equivalents." Scares also require an impending critical point beyond which remedial action is useless. This so-called "tipping point" is currently estimated to allow a drop of about 0.2 pH units, a value that could be reached in as near as 30 years. It is no surprise the author of these outrageous and incorrect remarks is chair of the EuroCLIMATE program Scientific Committee.

Current Changes Are Natural and Normal

A plot of CO_2 levels over the last 600 million years shows current levels are very low at 385 ppm.

The only period in 600 million years when CO_2 levels were equal to the present was over 300 million years ago. Since that time CO_2 levels averaged 1000 to 1200 ppm or 3 to 4 times current levels. How did the plant and animal life survive those levels? It makes a mockery of the claim that even a doubling of atmospheric CO_2 is a problem. . . .

Not Succumbing to Fear

Marie Curie, one of the greatest scientists of all time, said, "Nothing in life is to be feared. It is only to be understood." Gradually, more and more evidence shows the hypothesis that human CO_2 is causing warming or climate change is false. Fear is subsiding as more people, including many scientists, understand and are speaking out. A surprising one recently was Tom Tripp, a member and lead author of the IPCC since 2004. At the July 2009 Utah Farm Bureau Convention he said there is so much natural variability in weather [that] it makes a scientifically valid conclusion about man-made global warming difficult. Specifically, he said, "It may well be, but we're not scientifically there yet." That contradicts the message from the reports he helped author. It also disavows the claim that the science is settled. The outrage is [that] alarmists continue to present a message of certainty. However, just in case you are wavering, the sky is definitely falling and they will continue to produce outrageous unsubstantiated scares to prove it.

EVALUATING THE AUTHORS' ARGUMENTS:

Tim Ball, along with previous authors Marc Sheppard and Lorne Gunter, describes global warming advocates as "alarmists." Explain what is meant by this term. Why do you think Ball, Sheppard, and Gunter view their opponents as alarmist? In your opinion, do the other authors in this chapter, Mary Ann Whitley, Rob Young and Orrin Pilkey, and the Natural Resources Defense Council, qualify as alarmists? Write three to five paragraphs on what is meant by the term *environmental alarmist*. Then state whether you agree with or oppose this characterization of people who are concerned about climate change. Quote from at least three viewpoints in your answer.

Chapter 2

What Are the Most Significant Threats to Oceans?

A humpback whale is seen dragging a line and a plastic buoy that is lodged in its mouth. Many marine animals become snared in plastic garbage that litters the world's oceans.

Overfishing Is a Serious Threat to Oceans

Daniel Pauly

"It is not just the future of the fishing industry that is at stake, but also the continued health of the world's largest ecosystem."

In the following viewpoint Daniel Pauly warns that the ocean's fish stocks are in dire trouble. He explains that most of the world's large fish populations have been fished to the point of collapse. In fact, some reputable studies have predicted that by 2048 there will be so few fish in the ocean, it will be impossible to harvest them without driving populations to extinction. Should fish become extinct, millions of people who depend on them for food and income will suffer, he warns. In addition, the oceans will become lifeless dead zones that will contribute to climate change and environmental catastrophe. Pauly concludes that governments must intervene to make sure that all fish are caught sustainably and responsibly.

Pauly is a professor at the Fisheries Centre of the University of British Columbia and the principal investigator of its Sea Around Us Project.

AS YOU READ, CONSIDER THE FOLLOWING QUESTIONS:
1. What are slimehead and toothfish now known as, according to Pauly?
2. By what percentage have populations of large fish been reduced in the last fifty years, according to the author?
3. How many millions of people does Pauly say rely on fish as their main protein source?

Our oceans have been the victims of a giant Ponzi scheme, waged with Bernie Madoff[1]–like callousness by the world's fisheries. Beginning in the 1950s, as their operations became increasingly industrialized—with onboard refrigeration, acoustic fish-finders, and, later, GPS [global positioning systems]—they first depleted stocks of cod, hake, flounder, sole, and halibut in the Northern Hemisphere. As those stocks disappeared, the fleets moved southward, to the coasts of developing nations and, ultimately, all the way to the shores of Antarctica, searching for icefishes and rockcods, and, more recently, for small, shrimplike krill.

As the bounty of coastal waters dropped, fisheries moved further offshore, to deeper waters. And, finally, as the larger fish began to disappear, boats began to catch fish that were smaller and uglier— fish never before considered fit for human consumption. Many were renamed so that they could be marketed: The suspicious slimehead became the delicious orange roughy, while the worrisome Patagonian toothfish became the wholesome Chilean seabass. Others, like the homely hoki, were cut up so they could be sold sight-unseen as fish sticks and filets in fast-food restaurants and the frozen-food aisle. . . .

Fish Are on the Brink of Collapse

The jig, however, is nearly up. In 1950, the newly constituted Food and Agriculture Organization (FAO) of the United Nations estimated that, globally, we were catching about 20 million metric tons of fish (cod, mackerel, tuna, etc.) and invertebrates (lobster, squid, clams,

---

1. Madoff, former chair of the NASDAQ stock exchange, was convicted of stealing billions of dollars in a widespread fraudulent investment scheme known as a Ponzi scheme, named after Charles Ponzi, who, in 1920, was the first well-known US perpetrator of such a scheme.

etc.). That catch peaked at 90 million tons per year in the late 1980s, and it has been declining ever since. Much like Madoff's infamous operation, which required a constant influx of new investments to generate "revenue" for past investors, the global fishing-industrial complex has required a constant influx of new stocks to continue operation. Instead of restricting its catches so that fish can reproduce and maintain their populations, the industry has simply fished until a stock is depleted and then moved on to new or deeper waters, and to smaller and stranger fish. And, just as a Ponzi scheme will collapse once the pool of potential investors has been drained, so too will the fishing industry collapse as the oceans are drained of life.

Ocean Health at Stake

Unfortunately, it is not just the future of the fishing industry that is at stake, but also the continued health of the world's largest ecosystem. While the climate crisis gathers front-page attention on a regular basis, people—even those who profess great environmental consciousness—continue to eat fish as if it were a sustainable practice. But eating a tuna roll at a sushi restaurant should be considered no more environmentally benign than driving a Hummer or harpooning a manatee. In the past 50 years, we have reduced the populations of large commercial fish, such as bluefin tuna, cod, and other favorites, by a staggering 90 percent. One study, published in the prestigious journal *Science*, forecast that, by 2048, *all* commercial fish stocks will have "collapsed," meaning that they will be generating 10 percent or less of their peak catches. Whether or not that particular year, or even decade, is correct, one thing is clear: Fish are in dire peril, and, if they are, then so are we. . . .

Claims of Recovery Are Dubious

The notion that fish are globally imperiled has been challenged in many ways—perhaps most notably by fisheries biologists, who have questioned the facts, the tone, and even the integrity of those making such allegations. Fisheries biologists are different than marine ecologists like myself. Marine ecologists are concerned mainly with threats to the diversity of the ecosystems that they study, and so, they frequently work in concert with environmental NGOs [non-

A Chinese fishing fleet sets out for the China Sea. Overfishing and pollution have had a detrimental effect on the South China Sea's fisheries.

governmental organizations] and are often funded by philanthropic foundations. By contrast, fisheries biologists traditionally work for government agencies, like the National Marine Fisheries Service at the Commerce Department, or as consultants to the fishing industry, and their chief goal is to protect fisheries and the fishermen they employ. I myself was trained as a fisheries biologist in Germany, and, while they would dispute this, the agencies for which many of my former classmates work clearly have been captured by the industry they are supposed to regulate. Thus, there are fisheries scientists who, for example, write that cod have "recovered" or even "doubled" their numbers when, in fact, they have increased merely from 1 percent to 2 percent of their original abundance in the 1950s. . . .

The End of Fish Would Be Catastrophic

It is essential that we [rebuild fish populations] as quickly as possible because the consequences of an end to fish are frightful. To some Western nations, an end to fish might simply seem like a culinary catastrophe, but for 400 million people in developing nations, particularly

Overfishing Is a Serious Threat

Overfishing takes a toll on fisheries; data from the United Nations Environment Programme show that 70 percent are crashed or overexploited.

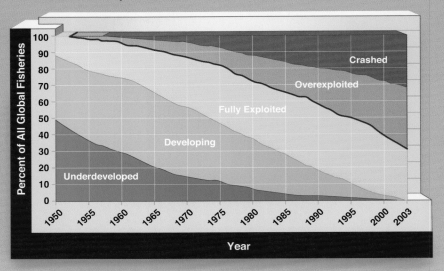

Taken from: Environmental Defense Fund, "Oceans of Abundance," 2008, p.4.

in poor African and South Asian countries, fish are the main source of animal protein. What's more, fisheries are a major source of livelihood for hundreds of million of people. A recent World Bank report found that the income of the world's 30 million small-scale fisheries is shrinking. The decrease in catch has also dealt a blow to a prime source of foreign-exchange earnings, on which impoverished countries, ranging from Senegal in West Africa to the Solomon Islands in the South Pacific, rely to support their imports of staples such as rice.

And, of course, the end of fish would disrupt marine ecosystems to an extent that we are only now beginning to appreciate. Thus, the removal of small fish in the Mediterranean to fatten bluefin tuna in pens is causing the "common" dolphin to become exceedingly rare in some areas, with local extinction probable. Other marine mammals and seabirds are similarly affected in various parts of the world. Moreover, the removal of top predators from marine ecosystems has effects that cascade down, leading to the increase of jellyfish and other gelatinous zooplankton and to the gradual erosion of the food web within which fish populations are embedded. This is what happened off the coast of southwestern Africa, where an upwelling ecosystem similar to that off California, previously dominated by fish such as hake and sardines, has become overrun by millions of tons of jellyfish.

A Watery Horror Show

Jellyfish population outbursts are also becoming more frequent in the northern Gulf of Mexico, where the fertilizer-laden runoff from the Mississippi River fuels uncontrolled algae blooms. The dead algae then fall to a sea bottom from which shrimp trawling has raked all animals capable of feeding on them, and so they rot, causing Massachusetts-sized "dead zones." Similar phenomena—which only jellyfish seem to enjoy—are occurring throughout the world, from the Baltic Sea to the Chesapeake Bay, and from the Black Sea in southeastern Europe to the Bohai Sea in northeastern China. Our oceans, having nourished us since the beginning of the human species some 150,000 years ago, are now turning against us, becoming angry opponents.

> **FAST FACT**
>
> The International Union for Conservation of Nature reported in 2008 that more than one-quarter of sharks and rays in the northeast Atlantic are threatened with extinction due to overfishing.

That dynamic will only grow more antagonistic as the oceans become warmer and more acidic because of climate change. Fish are expected to suffer mightily from global warming, making it essential that we preserve as great a number of fish and of fish species as possible, so that those which are able to adapt are around to evolve and propagate the next incarnations of marine life. In fact, new evidence tentatively suggests that large quantities of fish biomass could actually help attenuate ocean acidification. In other words, fish could help save us from the worst consequences of our own folly—yet we are killing them off. The jellyfish-ridden waters we're seeing now may be only the first scene in a watery horror show. . . .

Fishing Must Become Sustainable and Responsible

There is no need for an end to fish, or to fishing for that matter. But there is an urgent need for governments to free themselves from the fishing-industrial complex and its Ponzi scheme, to stop subsidizing the fishing-industrial complex and awarding it fishing rights, when it should in fact pay for the privilege to fish. If we can do this, then we will have fish forever.

EVALUATING THE AUTHOR'S ARGUMENTS:

In the viewpoint you just read, Daniel Pauly uses facts, statistics, examples, and reasoning to make his argument that the oceans are at risk of being overfished. He does not, however, use any quotations to support his point. If you were to rewrite this article and insert quotations, from what authorities might you quote? Where would you place the quotations, and why?

Viewpoint

2

The Threat of Overfishing Has Been Exaggerated

Nancy Gaines

> "[Fish] stocks 'are expected to continue to rebuild as a result of sustained fishing rates and successful fish reproduction.'"

In the following viewpoint Nancy Gaines argues that not all fish stocks are threatened by overfishing. In fact, Gaines argues, many fish stocks are healthy, stable, and on the brink of full recovery. Restrictions on fishing and other conservation measures have helped fish stocks rebound in recent years, she explains. But more than that, Gaines argues, many fish populations were never as imperiled as some scientists and government bodies would have people believe. She accuses these entities of exaggerating the threat to fish and of failing to take some areas into account when calculating fish populations. Gaines says it is alarmist and reckless to warn of the end of fish and concludes there is no reason to think any such scenario is likely to occur.

Gaines is a reporter whose articles have appeared in the *New York Times* and the *Boston Globe*.

AS YOU READ, CONSIDER THE FOLLOWING QUESTIONS:
1. Which fish species stock was expected to be completely rebuilt by 2011, according to Gaines?
2. What does the author say is the difference between being "over-fished" and "endangered"?
3. What, according to Gaines, is akin to the US Census Bureau's estimating the population but failing to include urban areas in its count?

The message that many environmentalists would have you believe is this: We're catching and eating the oceans bare.

"There is an end in sight" for fish, a 2006 *Science* magazine paper proclaimed. The paper even put a date to the end time: the year 2048.

The paper was produced by a team of scientists headed by Boris Worm, a professor at Dalhousie University in Nova Scotia.

Worm's idea that the world's supply of seafood would be exhausted within the lifetime of many alive today caused a sensation. The "2048" prediction gave it a news hook that made headlines around the world.

Scares About Fish Stocks Are Nothing New

The idea that the world's fisheries were on the verge of collapse was not new. In 1998, in another *Science* magazine article, University of British Columbia professor Daniel Pauly predicted overfishing would consume every species until nothing was left but "jellyfish and plankton soup."

A decade later, the same theme was sounded by "Oceans of Abundance," the 2008 policy paper prepared for the incoming administration of Barack Obama by a team convened by the Environmental Defense Fund, the leading advocate of the current catch share system of fisheries management.

The team included marine biologist Jane Lubchenco, who last year [in 2009] was picked by President Obama to head the National Atmospheric and Oceanic Administration [NOAA].

"Evidence is overwhelming," the policy paper said. "The global oceans are being emptied of seafood. . . . There is scientific consensus that fishing is fundamentally altering ocean ecosystems, which are increasingly likely to yield massive swarms of jellyfish rather than food fish."

That "scientific consensus" was the justification for the catch share system imposed on the New England fishery by Lubchenco as NOAA administrator.

In fact, the claim of a scientific consensus was as questionable as the claim that manmade global warming was "settled science."

Fish Stocks Are Healthy and Rebounding

Most New England fish stocks are healthy, stable and improving, according to NOAA's own figures, after more than a decade of management to rebuild the stocks.

Cod fills the hold of a fishing boat. The New England Fishery Council has said that depleted cod stocks in the North Atlantic were expected to be fully rebuilt by 2011.

"We've reduced fish mortality in most of the stocks," Steven Murawski, director of scientific programs and chief science adviser for NOAA's National Marine Fisheries Service, said in a recent interview. "We can't drain the pond and count, but the science is compelling."

Tom Nies, chief fishery analyst of the New England Fishery Management Council, said the rebuilding of imperiled stocks is on track or even ahead of schedule.

Cod, for example—often cited as a poster child for alleged over-fishing—is expected to be fully rebuilt by next year [2011], Nies said, perhaps this year [2010].

The rest of the stocks in the New England groundfishery are all at different points of recovery—but all are recovering.

Two hundred miles out, from the Canadian border down to Florida, under the belly of the nation, through the Gulf of Mexico and up the Pacific Coast to Alaska, the great American fishery is in no risk of dying.

That is what the latest stock data shows. What has been portrayed by some as a catastrophe in the making can be seen as an American success story.

Restrictions and Conservation Measures Have Worked

The waters of the Western Atlantic have been commercially fished since at least the 15th century. By the middle of the 20th century, human depredation had taken a heavy toll, requiring radical steps. New England fishermen have taken much of the blame for the over-fishing of the past and have paid the price.

Fishing restrictions have reduced the size of the fleet, and conservation policies limited the number of days the remaining boats can fish.

Now the fleet faces new restrictions under the catch share system imposed by Lubchenco. The system parcels out shares of a greatly reduced total catch.

Stephen Ouellette, an attorney and advocate for the local industry, argued in a research paper presented to government officials in March that the catch could be increased by 20 percent and still not threaten the recovery of the stocks, although he conceded it might take longer for stocks to completely rebuild.

Thirteen of 20 species of groundfish in New England waters are "overfished," as defined by regulators. That does not mean they are

Fisheries Are Bouncing Back

Of ten ecosystems studied, researchers found that the majority were being fished below their multispecies maximum yield, which gives ecosystems a chance to recover. At least five ecosystems were found to be recovering.

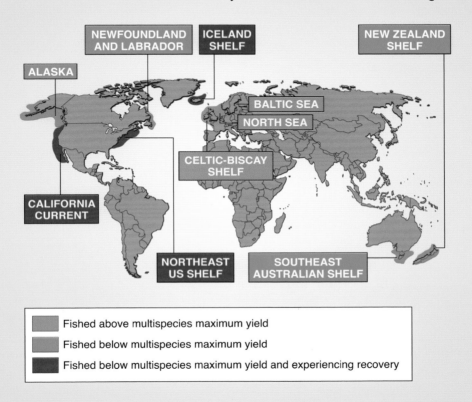

Fished above multispecies maximum yield

Fished below multispecies maximum yield

Fished below multispecies maximum yield and experiencing recovery

Taken from: Associated Press, "Sustainable Seas? Overfishing Easing in Places," July 31, 2009./Communication Partnership for Science and the Sea, 2009.

endangered, simply that the species has not yet achieved "optimal biomass"—a naturally sustainable population, though what constitutes a sustainable population is a moving, and controversial, target.

The tough restrictions on fishermen—plus nature's resilience—have brought the fish back.

"We had a big-year class of haddock (in 2009)," said Brian Rothschild, dean emeritus at the School for Marine Science and Technology at the University of Massachusetts Dartmouth.

"Scallops are in high abundance. But a lot of that is caused naturally, as is decline. Some abundance is hastened by fishery management, but the role of the natural environment is underplayed."

Some Populations Have Doubled, Even Tripled

Jim Balsiger, then NOAA's acting assistant administrator in charge of fisheries, noted in a [*Gloucester (MA)*] *Times* column last August [2009] that reduction of cod fishing in New England in recent years has contributed to a tripling of Gulf of Maine cod population since 1994—and a doubling of Georges Bank cod population since its low point in 2005.

Citing a 2009 study called "Rebuilding Global Fisheries," Balsiger noted that these stocks "are expected to continue to rebuild as a result of sustained fishing rates and successful fish reproduction. . . .

"All is not gloom and doom, there are some positive signs," Balsiger said. "The big story is that fisheries are still an important part of the economy. I am pretty optimistic for New England fish stocks."

Murawski, the National Marine Fisheries Service [NMFS] scientist, credits much of the comeback to the cooperation of the fishermen.

"We need to get over some sticky management and political issues," he says, "and align the interests of the fishermen and the science."

Selective Surveying Is Part of the Problem

Those interests are not yet aligned. The government's allocations for the new fishing year—which began May 1 [2010]—aim to further tighten the limits.

"The resource is exploding and the industry is going in a downward direction," Vito Giacalone, program director of the Gloucester-based Northeast Seafood Coalition, told the *Times* last month.

Fishermen have little faith in the government science behind the new limits.

New Jersey fisherman James Lovgren, who has worked with the Trawl Survey Advisory Panel to the New England Fishery Science Center—which provides the study data for the National Marine Fisheries Service, noted that, in studying flounder, NMFS canceled its annual winter survey.

That, he said, meant the flounder studies would miss "what every offshore fisherman from Massachusetts and Rhode island already knows—there is an enormous biomass of summer flounder that now spend the winter on the southern edges of the Georges Bank in 50 to 75 fathoms of water."

Lovgren also said federal regulators neglected to sample Nantucket Shoals, where a large portion of the blackback and yellowtail flounder live.

"This selective surveying," he wrote, "is equivalent to the U.S. Census Bureau estimating the population, but not including all urban areas."

Scientists Publishing for Publicity's Sake

The science that was used to justify the new catch shares regime is disputed not only by fishermen but also by many scientists.

A landmark 2006 essay in *Fisheries Magazine* called "Faith-based Fisheries" took on the notion that fisheries management techniques have failed and new, more radical steps are needed to protect fish.

The author was Ray Hilborn, an oft-published professor of fish management at the University of Washington in Seattle.

He compared agenda-driven fisheries scientists to "creationists" who deny the reality of evolution and tailor their science to fit their preconceived ideas.

"I suggest," Hilborn wrote, "the fisheries community needs to look at itself and question whether there is not within our own field a strong movement of faith-based acceptance of ideas, and a search for data to support these ideas."

> **FAST FACT**
>
> A 2009 study in the journal *Science* found that of ten areas examined around the world, two had no overfishing problem and five had taken steps to control overfishing.

Hilborn also accused the science journals *Science* and *Nature* of publishing a string of papers on the collapse of the fisheries, "not for their scientific merit, but for their publicity value."

"I assert that . . . many of these papers are being published only because the editors and selected reviewers believe in the message, or because of their potential newsworthiness."

Worm himself inadvertently admitted that his prediction of a fisheries collapse by 2048 was meant to capture headlines.

Shortly after the paper was published in *Science*, Worm said in an e-mail he accidentally sent to the *Seattle Times* that he put in the doomsday date as a "news hook."

Reckless Warnings

It caught on in the popular press and, coming out at a time that Congress was debating a rewrite of the Magnuson-Stevens Act regulating fishing, was used to push the idea that tough new rules were needed.

But many scientists were skeptical of Worm's analysis.

Papers that reference the 2048 date are "reckless," says Rothschild of UMass [University of Massachusets], "and there is scientific consensus that they are."

Another critic of Worm's 2048 doomsday date was Murawski, the Fisheries Service scientist. Murawski debunked Worm's alarmist assertion in a lecture on sustainable fisheries he delivered at Yale University in 2007.

Murawski said a flawed analysis caused Worm to count recovering stocks as collapsed stocks, then extrapolate those figures into the future.

The sky was really not falling into a sterile sea.

EVALUATING THE AUTHORS' ARGUMENTS:

In this viewpoint Nancy Gaines argues that some fish populations—such as cod—have doubled, even tripled. How would Daniel Pauly, author of the previous viewpoint, respond to this argument? With which author do you ultimately agree on this point? Explain your reasoning.

Fish Farming Threatens Ocean Fish Stocks

> *"The escape of farmed Pacific and Atlantic salmon into wild salmon habitat poses a serious threat to indigenous wild Pacific salmon."*

Coastal Alliance for Aquaculture Reform

The Coastal Alliance for Aquaculture Reform (CAAR) is an organization that works to protect wild salmon, coastal communities, and ecosystems from fish farming. In the following viewpoint the alliance explains the ways in which fish farming threatens wild fish populations. Farmed fish lessen the catch of wild fish because farmed fish are fed wild fish, contends the author. Furthermore, farmed fish are given large quantities of antibiotics and vaccines, which pollute the water. CAAR also says that fish-farm pens are a breeding ground for sea lice, which feed on and cause disease in wild salmon. Finally, CAAR warns that farmed fish often escape from their pens; when they do, they compete with wild fish for food and breed with wild fish. For all of these reasons, CAAR concludes fish farming should be abolished because of its threat to wild fish populations.

AS YOU READ, CONSIDER THE FOLLOWING QUESTIONS:
  1. What percentage of migrating juvenile salmon does CAAR say can be infected by sea lice from farmed fish pens?
  2. What is infectious salmon anemia and how does it factor into the author's argument?
  3. How many kilometers away from their pens have escaped farmed salmon been found, according to CAAR?

S almon farming is one of the most harmful aquaculture production systems.

The industry uses open net-cages placed directly in the ocean, where farm waste, chemicals, disease and parasites are released directly into the surrounding waters, harming other marine life. Escapes of thousands of farmed fish are common in the industry, as are the death of natural predators like sea lions and seals who are attracted to the pens of fish.

Farmed Fish Eat Wild Fish and Cause Disease

Raising carnivorous fish like salmon that require a high percentage of protein derived from wild fish in their feed also has a significant impact on the environment. More kilograms of wild fish are used to raise salmon than farmed salmon produced, depleting wild fish stocks rather than supplementing them.

The vast majority of salmon farming operations depend on the use of vaccines, antibiotics and pesticides to control disease and parasites that are often exacerbated by the high densities required to make industrial livestock operations profitable.

One of the most devastating impacts of salmon farming is the risk sea lice pose to juvenile wild salmon. Sea lice proliferate on salmon farms and spread to surrounding waters attacking baby salmon as they head out to sea. . . .

When over half a million or more farmed salmon are penned in a small area, fish feces and waste feed can have a significant impact on the ocean bottom and surrounding ecosystems, especially in shallow waters or areas that do not flush well. . . .

Despite regulations and management practices intended to limit farmed salmon escapes, escapes still happen in every salmon farming region in the world. . . .

Open net-cages attract natural fish-eating predators like seals and sea lions. Some of these marine mammals are shot by fish farmers that feel that the animals are a threat to their stock. Others become ensnared in the nets surrounding the open net-cages and drown. An untold number of seals, sea lions, dolphins and porpoises are killed annually by salmon farms. . . .

The Threat from Sea Lice

Sea lice from salmon farms are one of the most significant threats facing wild salmon in British Columbia [BC]. Although sea lice occur naturally, lice infestations have only recently put wild salmon populations at risk. In the spring, fish eggs hatch and juvenile salmon emerge from the rivers and make their way to the ocean estuaries and bays. It is primarily when young salmon fry migrate past salmon farms that they encounter large concentrations of sea lice. When these large concentrations of lice attach themselves to juveniles, their bodies may not be able to cope, and they may die.

Stocking hundreds of thousands of fish in small areas (net-pens) makes fish farms ideal and unnatural breeding grounds for lice. This significantly increases the number of lice in surrounding waters and the threat to out-migrating wild juvenile salmon.

- Farmed fish make great hosts for sea lice because they are confined and in high densities.
- 91% of BC's farmed salmon are the non-native Atlantic species, which are more susceptible to sea lice than many other salmon species.
- Research experiments have shown that pink and chum salmon fry can die when infected with only a single mature sea louse, and data suggests that up to 95% of migrating juvenile salmon can be infected.
- Current chemical treatment of sea lice on farms may be harmful to other marine species and may not reduce lice levels enough to protect wild salmon. . . .

A man holds a vial containing a salmon fry infested with sea lice. Sea lice proliferate in salmon farms and spread to surrounding waters, attacking wild baby salmon as they head out to sea.

A Vector for Disease

A growing body of peer-reviewed research published in prestigious science journals indicates that sea lice are dangerous to juvenile wild salmon.

Sea lice feed on the mucus, blood and skin of salmon. While a few lice on a large salmon may not cause serious damage, large numbers of lice on that same fish, or just a couple of lice on a juvenile salmon, can be harmful or fatal. The feeding activity of sea lice can cause serious fin damage, skin erosion, constant bleeding, and deep open wounds creating a pathway for other pathogens.

It is also possible for sea lice to carry diseases between farmed and wild salmon. This disease "vector" has already been shown for Infectious Salmon Anemia (ISA) on the Atlantic coast. An outbreak of ISA on salmon farms in Chile in late fall, 2007 spread rapidly from one farm to the next, leading to whole pens and in one case an entire farm's worth of fish having to be destroyed. Sea lice have been identified as a possible factor in the rapid spread of the disease.

The furunculosis bacterium has also been found on the bodies of sea lice, making it likely that sea lice spread this disease as well.

Farmed Salmon Could Lead to Extinction of Wild Populations

Cutting edge research published in the prestigious journal *Science* in December, 2007 was the first study to calculate the impact individual wild salmon mortalities from sea lice infestation can have on the population of a whole run of salmon. The recurrent louse infestations associated with salmon farms in BC's Broughton Archipelago have depressed wild pink salmon populations there and placed them on a trajectory toward rapid local extinction. The *Science* study shows louse-induced mortality of pink salmon is commonly over 80% and exceeds previous fishing mortality. The study concludes:

> **FAST FACT**
>
> A 2010 report published in the *Canadian Journal of Fisheries and Aquatic Sciences* found nearby salmon farms to be a major source of sea lice found in wild juvenile salmon.

- If outbreaks continue, a 99% collapse in pink salmon population abundance is expected within two salmon generations (four years) from the study's publication date and local extinction is predicted.
- A 99% population collapse means, in just four short years, the pink salmon runs in the area will disappear, impacting the bears,

orcas (killer whales), eagles, seals, sea lions and fish species that they sustain.

- The decaying bodies of salmon also fertilize riparian (stream-side) forests, contribute to nutrients and feed coastal food webs. The loss of pink salmon populations will erode the entire coastal ecosystem, threatening the survival of not only the flora and fauna but also the communities and economies that depend on these resources. . . .

The Threat from Escaped Salmon

The escape of farmed Pacific and Atlantic salmon into wild salmon habitat poses a serious threat to indigenous wild Pacific salmon. Escapes have the potential to out-compete wild salmon for habitat and food and spread disease and pathogens to wild fish.

The WWF [World Wildlife Fund] Salmon Aquaculture Dialogue Report on Escapes found that escaped farmed salmon "are usually recorded within 500 km of the escape site, but have been recorded up to 2,000–4,500 km from the escape/release site."

The Atlantic Salmon Watch Program (ASWP), a cooperative research program operated by the Department of Fisheries and Oceans (DFO) and BC's Ministry of Agriculture and Lands (BCMAL), conducted monitoring and removal of escaped Atlantic salmon from streams. While operational, this program suggested that there have been cases of escaped farmed Atlantic salmon surviving and then breeding with other escaped Atlantic salmon in BC streams. However, the program has been abandoned and is no longer functional beyond a webpage and phone number and it has been reported that messages left at this number typically receive no response.

A study published in *Conservation Biology* reported that non-native Atlantic salmon were found in over 80 wild salmon spawning streams in British Columbia, with feral juvenile Atlantic salmon having been discovered at three locations. However, very little research has been done with regards to the extent of Atlantic salmon populations in BC rivers today.

According to the Ministry of Agriculture and Lands (BCMAL), the agency responsible for tracking industry-reported farmed salm-

Farmed Fish May Escape

Data from the Norwegian Directorate of Fisheries show that hundreds of thousands of farmed salmon escape their pens each year. These salmon compete with wild salmon for food and breed with them, threatening the wild population.

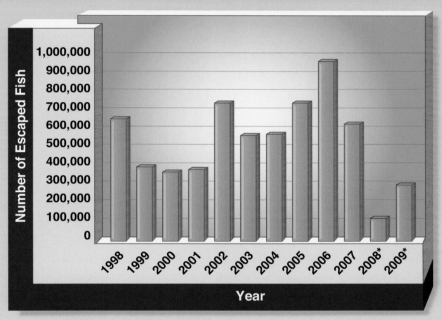

Escapes of Farmed Salmonids

*Preliminary numbers that will be updated
The amount for 2009 shows reported escapes until October 5, 2009

Taken from: Bellona Aqua Web, "Escaped Farmed Fish," October 15, 2009. www.bellona.org.

on escapes, over 1.5 million farmed salmon escaped into BC waters between 1987 and 2008. Escapes were due to system failure related to extreme weather, net tears or structural damage resulting from propeller or boat collision with the nets, attacks by predators such as seals and sea lions or through human error and vandalism.

EVALUATING THE AUTHORS' ARGUMENTS:

The Coastal Alliance for Aquaculture Reform argues that farmed salmon reduce populations of wild fish by requiring wild fish for their feed. How would *Global Agenda,* the author of the following viewpoint, suggest this problem be solved? With which author do you ultimately agree—does fish farming protect or threaten wild fish populations? What evidence swayed you?

Fish Farming Need Not Threaten Ocean Fish Stocks

Global Agenda

"Problems seem likely to worsen as fish farming grows. But there are solutions."

In the following editorial published by the editors of *Global Agenda,* the authors argue that although fish farming poses some threat to wild fish stocks, these problems can be overcome, and fish farming can ultimately help save wild fish stocks. Although salmon pens attract parasites and disease, the authors suggest moving them away from wild salmon runs or even raising them in inland ponds. They also suggest solving the problem of using wild fish to feed farmed fish by encouraging fish farmers to raise vegetarian breeds of fish. The authors argue that only fish farming can satisfy the world's insatiable appetite for fish: Wild fish will be driven to extinction if they are expected to meet the growing worldwide demand for fish. The authors conclude that fish farming is a young industry that needs more time to work out its kinks. When these problems are solved, fish farming will help protect wild fish populations. *Global Agenda* is an annual publication of the Economist Newspaper Ltd., a British periodical publisher.

AS YOU READ, CONSIDER THE FOLLOWING QUESTIONS:
1. How many extra tons of fish will be needed to maintain current levels of consumption by 2030, according to the authors?
2. What benefit is there to farm-raising tilapia and catfish, according to *Global Agenda*?
3. What is OceanBoy Farms and how does it factor into the authors' argument?

The world needs more farmed fish

MANKIND'S transition from hunting and gathering to farming began about 12,000 years ago, when people decided to stay put and cultivate the plants they liked. Although people have since domesticated a vast array of the world's animals and plants, in one area at least we have never really shaken off our hunter-gatherer roots. Most of our fish is still caught in the wild, much as it was in our ancestors' time—albeit with a few more fancy bits of gadgetry to tip the balance in favour of the hunter, rather than the gathered.

> **FAST FACT**
>
> A 2007 report by the Ministry of Agriculture and Lands in British Columbia, Canada, stated that no diseases were found in salmon farms that had not already been reported in the wild.

The thrill of the chase, though, may increasingly be a thing of the past. Fish farming has been the world's fastest growing food-production sector, with output rising 8.8% a year since 1970, according to the Food and Agriculture Organisation. By comparison, livestock production increased at a rate of 2.8% a year. Today, some 45% of all fish consumed by humans—around 48m tonnes—is raised on farms. That is still only half of what is caught in the ocean (much of which goes to feed livestock), but at this rate, in eight years farming will produce as many fish as are caught at sea today.

Levels of wild-fish catches have been stable since the mid-1980s, and the vast majority of the world's capture-fisheries are fully exploited—or indeed over-exploited: we cannot, therefore, catch more wild fish than we do today. But the demand for fish is booming, thanks to growing numbers of people, and their increasing affluence.

By 2030 a whopping 37m extra tonnes of fish will be needed to maintain current levels of fish consumption per person. The missing fish that needs to be found to sustain levels of consumption has been dubbed the "fish gap", and it will have to be filled by fish farming. But fish farming has its problems, too. It does not, for instance, always increase the total amount of fish available. Carnivorous farmed fish must be fed wild fish; for every pound of salmon eaten, several pounds of wild fish must be caught. Currently, much of this fishmeal can be obtained by using industrially caught fish to feed fish rather than animals, but what happens after that?

Bluefin tuna swim in a Mediterranean fish farm. The author argues that fish farming is the only way to sustain the world's voracious appetite for fish.

Farmed Fish Is the Only Way to Meet Demand

Farmed seafood provides nearly half of the world's seafood supply, and the industry is growing. Supporters say that farming fish is the only way to meet increasing world demand for fish without emptying the seas.

World Aquaculture Production, 1950–2006

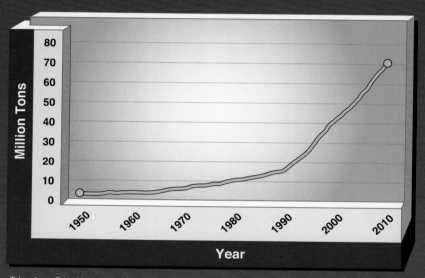

Taken from: Brian Halweil, "Farming Fish for the Future," World Watch Institute, vol. 176, September 2008.

Fish farming already uses up most of the world's fish oil and a hefty chunk of its fish meal.

Many aquaculturists are now eyeing krill, a small crustacean found in the cold waters of Antarctica. It is an excellent source of nutrition for farmed fish. Unfortunately, krill is central to the Antarctic marine food-web, and it is also an excellent source of nutrition for all of the species in the Southern Ocean.

Another problem with salmon farming has been revealed in a recent paper that shows the damage salmon farms can do to nearby wild fish populations. Farmed salmon, kept in unnaturally high densities, are a breeding ground for parasitic sea lice. When young wild salmon on their way to the ocean swim past pens of farmed salmon at the mouths of rivers, they get infested with these lice. The scientists say that lice infestations could drive some salmon populations they studied in British Columbia to extinction in four years.

Such problems seem likely to worsen as fish farming grows. But there are solutions. One is to farm more vegetarian fish such as tilapia and catfish. Another is to move salmon pens to better locations. Earlier this year, John Fredriksen, the main shareholder in Marine Harvest, the world's largest salmon farming company, said that salmon farms ought to be moved away from wild salmon runs.

A better, although more expensive, solution would be to make fish farms self-contained. OceanBoy Farms, a company in Florida, produces organic inland shrimp using cleverly designed ponds that avoid

Top Aquaculture Species Used in Fish Farming

Species (y-axis): Japanese kelp, Pacific cupped oyster, Silver carp, Grass carp, Common carp, Japanese carpet shell, Bighead carp, Wakame, Whiteleg shrimp, Crucian carp, Nile tilapia, Laver (Nori)

Production (million tons)

Taken from: Brian Halweil, "Farming Fish for the Future," World Watch Institute, vol. 176, September 2008, pp. 8–9.

another environmental side-effect of fish-farming—the dumping of fish faeces and uneaten food onto the bottoms of sensitive marine environments, such as Scottish lochs. Some have linked this filth to the growth of toxic algal blooms.

Compared to terrestrial agriculture, fish farming is young, and it has a lot of growing up to do. Like farming, it causes environmental problems but offers great benefits. The world will have to find solutions to the first in order properly to enjoy the second.

EVALUATING THE AUTHORS' ARGUMENTS:

To make their argument in this viewpoint, the editors of *Global Agenda* discuss the transition from hunting and gathering to agricultural farming. What point do they make on this issue? How does this factor into the argument about fish farming? In your opinion, is this a good argument for why fish farming should be pursued? Why or why not?

Plastic Waste in the Oceans Poses a Serious Threat

Ed Cumming

"The ocean will continue to bear the brunt of our wasteful ways with plastic."

Ed Cumming is a British journalist and writer whose articles have appeared in London's *Daily Telegraph* newspaper and other British publications. In the following viewpoint he argues that plastic waste in the world's oceans poses a serious threat to both marine and human life. Cumming explains that plastic waste is ending up in the oceans at an alarming rate. In fact, there is more plastic in the oceans than some forms of marine life. In the ocean, plastic breaks into tiny pieces and photodegrades, a process that releases toxins into the water. These small pieces and toxins are absorbed or eaten by marine life, which then pollute people who eat fish. Larger pieces of plastic strangle, maim, and otherwise threaten birds and mammals. Cumming concludes that it is nearly impossible to remove plastic waste from the world's oceans, where it is doing increasing amounts of damage.

AS YOU READ, CONSIDER THE FOLLOWING QUESTIONS:
1. How big is the Great Pacific Garbage Patch estimated to be, according to Cumming?
2. According to the author, how much more plastic is in the ocean than plankton?
3. How many birds and mammals does Cumming say die each year from plastics?

The world's biggest rubbish dump keeps growing. The Great Pacific Garbage Patch—or the Pacific Trash Vortex—is a floating monument to our culture of waste, the final resting place of every forgotten carrier [grocery] bag, every discarded bottle and every piece of packaging blown away in the wind. Opinions about the exact size of this great, soupy mix vary, but some claim it has doubled over the past decade, making it now six times the size of the UK [United Kingdom].

Dr Simon Boxall, a physical oceanographer at the National Oceanography Centre at the University of Southampton, goes even further: "It's the size of North America. But although the patch itself is extremely large, it's only one very clear representation of the much bigger worldwide problem."

Plastic Is Polluting Our Oceans

This global problem is the motive behind the *Plastiki*, a 60ft, 12-ton catamaran built from 12,500 recycled plastic bottles, which embarks on its maiden voyage from San Francisco this week [March 2010]. The brainchild of David de Rothschild, the flamboyant British banking heir and environmentalist, the *Plastiki* will sail right through the middle of the Garbage Patch as part of a campaign to help make more people aware of the Pacific's threatened communities and of the damage our waste is doing to our oceans.

Plastic is the main issue. Fifty years ago, most flotsam was biodegradable. Now it is 90 per cent plastic. In 2006, the United Nations Environment Programme estimated that there were 46,000 pieces of floating plastic in every square mile of ocean. With its stubborn refusal to biodegrade, all plastic not buried in landfills—roughly half of it—sweeps into streams and sewers and then out into rivers and, finally, the ocean. Some of it—some say as much as 70 per cent—sinks to the ocean floor. The remainder floats, usually within 20 metres of the surface, and is carried into stable circular currents, or gyres "like ocean ring-roads," says Dr Boxall. Once inside these gyres, the plastic is drawn by wind and surface currents towards the centre, where it steadily accumulates. The world's major oceans all have these

The Plastiki, *a boat made from 12,500 plastic bottles, arrives in Sydney, Australia, after completing a 7,990-mile voyage across the Pacific—including passage through the Great Pacific Garbage Patch—in an effort to raise public awareness of this issue.*

gyres, and all are gathering rubbish. Although the North Pacific—bordering California, Japan and China—is the biggest, there are also increasingly prominent gyres in the South Pacific, the North and South Atlantic and the Indian Oceans. Our problems with plastics are only just beginning.

More Plastic than Plankton

The Pacific Garbage Patch had been predicted as early as the late Eighties but it was only formally discovered in 1997 by Charles Moore, an American yacht-racing captain sailing home across the North Pacific from a competition in Hawaii. He noticed a large amount of debris in the centre of the gyre, and together with the oceanographer Curtis Ebbesmeyer, formulated the idea of the Eastern Garbage Patch. Other research revealed a secondary patch to the West, and these two together constitute the Great Pacific Patch. . . . In 1999, Moore followed up his initial findings with a report showing that there was eight times as much plastic as plankton in the North Pacific. And there is a lot of plankton.

FAST FACT

The United Nations Environment Programme reports that there are an estimated forty-six thousand pieces of plastic litter floating on every square mile of ocean.

The image of a great floating mound of trash, though evocative, can be misleading. Dr Boxall says: "People imagine it as a kind of football pitch [field] of rubbish you can go and walk on—it's not like that." As most of the plastic has been broken down into tiny particles, floating beneath the surface, it is impossible to photograph from aircraft or satellites, or even really to see until you are right in its centre. As a result, it is difficult to convey the grave danger this 100 million tons or so of rubbish—and counting—presents. This is where the *Plastiki*—named after [explorer] Thor Heyerdahl's *Kon-Tiki* project in 1947—comes in. Its crew of six is being skippered by the rising star of British ocean sailing, Jo Royle, 29. Ms Royle is everything you could want at the figurehead of your mission: blonde, vivacious and—behind a Lancastrian burr

Ocean Currents and the Great Pacific Garbage Patch

Several ocean currents contribute to the formation of the Great Pacific Garbage Patch in the Pacific Ocean.

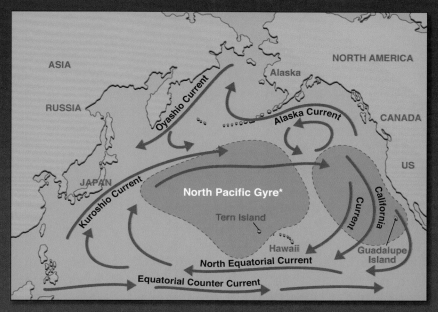

ASIA

NORTH AMERICA

Alaska

RUSSIA

Oyashio Current

Alaska Current

CANADA

JAPAN

Kuroshio Current

US

North Pacific Gyre*

California Current

Tern Island

Hawaii

Guadalupe Island

North Equatorial Current

Equatorial Counter Current

*A ringlike system of ocean currents

Taken from: Canadian Museum of Nature, 2009.

[regional accent] that survived her upbringing in Devon—a passionate environmentalist. She seems unfazed about sailing slap bang into the middle of the watery skip of the world.

"I can't wait to get there," she says. "Being in the middle of the ocean puts you back in your place—if you're not responsive, you don't survive. It makes you think hard about how you consume."

Plastic Toxins Enter the Food Chain

However, she readily concedes that it is easy for the layman to ask: "So what?" Some might be tempted to argue that the rubbish has to end up somewhere, and that the ocean is no worse than landfill. Herein lies the main danger: plastic does not biodegrade, but when exposed to sunlight it photo-degrades, breaking down into smaller and smaller particles, and finally to "nurdles," the industry name for the tiny grains that are the building blocks of most modern plastics. These tiny particles are not harmful on their own, but they are very absorbent, and soak up waterborne toxins, such as pesticides and cooling agents. These nurdles, now saturated in poisons, are eaten by filter-feeders at the very bottom of the food chain, and then make their way up it.

The scale of the toxin problem is unknown. Although plastics have now been around for a century, their use has only been really widespread for 50 years. Also, the threat is not only from food—marine extracts are used in countless other products too: particularly cosmetics. Since there are so many possible routes for toxins from these plastics to enter our food chain, there has yet to be an in-depth scientific study of their possible effect on humans. But these particles are certainly killing marine life: the UN estimates that more than one million birds and 100,000 mammals die every year from plastics—by poisoning, entanglement and choking. There are also studies under way investigating the possible connection between a rise in fertility problems and cancers, and the proliferation of plastic in the ocean.

A Bleak Outlook

The solution is equally confounding—there is just so much junk. Most experts agree that the real change needs to come above ground, from people taking more responsibility for their dumping.

As Ms Royle says: "The four worst-offending plastics—carrier bags, bottle-tops, bottles and styrofoam—are some we could easily do without, with a bit more thought. It's just about making the effort to change our habits: not getting chips [french fries] in a styrofoam container, reusing carrier bags—small things."

There are some—led by the renowned American environmentalist and National Geographic Explorer-at-large Sylvia Earle—who think that we should simply try not to use plastics at all. Ms Royle dismisses this approach: "Plastic is a part of our world, and it's hugely important."

Others would like the US government to embark on an operation to clean the ocean manually, using tankers to retrieve the plastic, which could then be used as fuel.

"I don't think that's a very good idea," says Ms Royle. "It would take a tremendous amount of resources to sweep the ocean. If you then burn the plastic, you create a lot of black carbon dioxide, which pollutes the atmosphere. I think the solution has to come from the shore." She points out that San Francisco, the city closest to the Great Pacific Patch, has successfully implemented policies to stop people using wasteful plastics. "If they can do it, so can we. We just need to stop all this dumb usage."

Dr Boxall is decidedly less optimistic: "There is nothing we can do," he says. "It's too big. It's here to stay. It's like nuclear waste. Even an oil spillage, disastrous as it is, eventually breaks down. Plastic doesn't. We've simply got to become better about how we dispose of waste."

The *Plastiki* team hopes its voyage can make a difference, however small. But until something drastically changes—particularly in developing countries, such as China and Brazil—the ocean will continue to bear the brunt of our wasteful ways with plastic. The Great Pacific Garbage Patch, and its growing imitators around the world, will continue to sprawl.

EVALUATING THE AUTHORS' ARGUMENTS:

Ed Cumming claims there is eight times as much plastic in the ocean as there is plankton. What does Martin Robbins, author of the following viewpoint, say about this claim? Write one paragraph that summarizes each author's position. Then, state with which author you ultimately agree on the issue of plastic waste in the ocean. Is it a serious threat, or has the threat been overstated?

The Threat from Plastic Waste in the Oceans Has Been Exaggerated

Martin Robbins

Journalists and environmentalists have greatly exaggerated the claim that plastic waste is polluting the ocean, argues Martin Robbins in the following viewpoint. Robbins contends that it is misleading to characterize trash in the ocean as an eighth continent, as some environmentalists have done. We cannot know how much plastic is in the ocean, and so Robbins says it is impossible to say whether it is growing. He also maintains that there is little evidence to show that plastic in the oceans negatively impacts marine life to the extent that environmentalists claim. Robbins agrees that plastic should not be dumped in the ocean but resents the lengths that environmentalists go to when stating the problem. He concludes that those who exaggerate the

"Assertion[s] that the Texas-sized trash vortex [in the Pacific Ocean] 'doubles in size every decade' is at best unevidenced and at worst made-up."

Martin Robbins, "The Great Pacific Garbage Patch: Fact vs. Fiction," Layscientist.net, November 13, 2009. Copyright © 2009 by The Lay Scientist. All rights reserved. Reprinted by permission.

problem of plastic waste in the oceans contribute to misinformation and hysteria about the problem. Robbins, a researcher and science writer, edits the blog Layscience.net.

AS YOU READ, CONSIDER THE FOLLOWING QUESTIONS:
1. Who is Lindsay Hoshaw and how does she factor into the author's argument?
2. Why, in Robbins's opinion, is it disingenuous to say that there is more plastic than plankton in the Pacific Ocean?
3. What does the author say the Sea Education Association has found after twenty-two years of research on plastic in the ocean?

As a keen supporter of the environment myself, one of the biggest problems with the environmental movement is a tendency to exaggerate. One of the worst examples of this right now surrounds Project Karsei, an expedition to the "Great Pacific Garbage Patch" or the "Pacific Trash Vortex," the uncritical reporting of which tends to be riddled with questionable science and statistics.

Judging by the experience of other writers tackling this subject, I'm probably going to get some flak for this, so I'll metaphorically duck behind senior Greenpeace scientist David Santillo, who has said: "The problem with superlative statements that this is somehow a huge floating mass of plastic is that they inevitably lead to desensitizing people when they learn the truth of it."

Absurd Claims and Huge Exaggerations
And the superlatives come thick and fast. The Ocean Voyages Institute ludicrously talk with almost religious fervour of

> . . . the plastics which are converging in the Pacific ocean and forming an 8th continent. Never heard of it? You need to help us. This is a rescue mission designed to save the Pacific by mining plastic. This 8th Continent has been identified northeast of Hawaii in the Pacific. Sailors and scientists, fishers and individuals have watched with horror, as this new continent comprised

of human discards, primarily plastic garbage, has grown and expanded exponentially over the last few years. Also called the plastic vortex, this 8th continent is currently twice the size of Texas and growing.

Environmentalist David Suzuki talks of "a massive, expanding island of plastic debris 30 metres deep and bigger than the province of Quebec," while Greenpeace themselves—no [strangers] to exaggeration—describe "one of the world's largest floating garbage dumps." Newspaper reports sourced talk of there being six-to-eight times more plastic than plankton.

Some of these claims are obviously absurd—an 8th continent?!—but as John Zhu has eloquently pointed out, journalists reporting on the "trash vortex" have failed to really challenge the people they're reporting on, or draw on research to add context to their efforts.

FAST FACT

After a 2008 scientific expedition to survey plastic debris in the Pacific Ocean, Angelicque White of Oregon State University announced that the floating garbage patch previously reported in the media to be twice the size of Texas is actually only about 1 percent the size of Texas.

Bad Journalism Abounds on This Issue

In particular, a debate has sprung up recently around the reporting of Lindsay Hoshaw, a Spot.us community-sponsored journalist whose report on Project Karsei—an environmentalist research project sailing in the region—ended up in the *New York Times*.

The Spot.us community paid Lindsay Hoshaw $10,000 to visit the region, but appear to have received little in the way of incisive journalism for their money, with the result coming across as a fairly uncritical travel blog. Should they have sent her in the first place? Zhu makes the following excellent point:

> Maybe instead of paying for someone to go take pictures of the patch, that $10,000 should go to paying for a reporter to sit

in a room somewhere, sift through reams of research data on the subject, visit fisheries, interview scientists, doctors, policy makers . . . It's not as exciting as a trip to the garbage patch and certainly lacks that "once-in-a-lifetime" appeal, but it may be the better route toward actually getting good journalism on the subject.

Exactly.

Misleading Statements Exaggerate the Problem

Which brings me neatly to the science itself. I'm not an ocean scientist, but I do have some experience of ocean modelling, and many of the claims being made ring alarm bells.

Let's take the comparison with plankton first. When somebody makes the claim that there is x times more plastic than plankton, the obvious first question any journalist should ask is "well how much plankton is there?" . . .

Some areas of the central Pacific have almost *100x* less plankton than, say, the North Atlantic does, and as much as *5,000x* less than parts of the Baltic Sea or English Channel.

Plankton don't generally live in great quantities in the middle of oceans, so saying that there are "x" lbs of plastic vs "x" lbs of plankton is a bit like seeing a washing machine dumped in the middle of the Sahara and returning home to announce that washing machine parts outnumber grass in parts of the desert.

There are (comparatively) sod-all [no] plankton in the mid-Pacific, and six times sod-all is still sod-all, a point starkly made by Greenpeace's own data, when they compile a table of the relative plastic content of the world's seas and oceans.

It should be noted that these are figures from visual inspection, and the amount of plastic that can be caught by nets may be far higher, but the point remains that there are other places with a far greater quantity of surface plastic than the North Pacific, making it frankly puzzling that just so much attention has been devoted to surface plastic in this area. Indeed, we can look at lot closer to home, at the English Channel, to find far more concerning levels of contamination that are orders of magnitude higher.

Garbage Patch Not Necessarily Growing

This is not to say that regions of high plastic contamination don't exist in the Pacific. Indeed, the NOAA [National Oceanic and Atmospheric Administration] describe two areas in the Pacific, the North Pacific Subtropical High and the North Pacific Subtropical Convergence Zone (STCZ) (media reports generally refer to the former). The size of these areas though is highly variable, and unknown, meaning that guesstimates by activists should be taken with a pinch of salt.

It is therefore not at all clear that these patches are growing, and Hoshaw's assertion that the Texas-sized trash vortex "doubles in size every decade" is at best unevidenced and at worst made-up.

In the Atlantic, attempts to measure growth have been inconclusive. The Sea Education Association have got 22 years' worth of data on the North Atlantic and Carribean, centering on a high plastic concentration at about thirty degrees north. The interesting thing from their data is that the quantity of plastic found hasn't increased in the 22 years they've been measuring it. That doesn't mean there isn't more there somewhere, but certainly something curious is happening to it.

Researchers with that group describe the phenomenon as a "plastic soup," a much more appropriate description and in some ways more alarming: "It's much worse. If it were an island, we could go get it. But we can't, because it's a thin soup of plastic fragments."

Effects on Marine Life Unclear

Even the effects of the plastic on life are not as clear-cut as reports would suggest. We know that many animals ingest small particles of plastic, but the end result of this is unclear and probably depends on the species. It is easy to post a photo of a dead chick with plastic in its stomach, and claim that the plastic was the cause of death; but far harder to back this up with evidence. Indeed, studies of albatross chick mortality in Hawaii in the late-1980s found no evidence of plastic related mortality.

It's additionally worth bearing in mind the vagueness about where these photos were taken, and the lack of experimental rigour inherent in surveying contents by taking random photos. Personally I do

A penguin lies strangled in a discarded canned-drink holder. Some say that environmentalists and journalists are exaggerating the extent of plastic in the ocean.

believe plastic is likely to poison or kill some life, but we need more information about the precise extent. As shocking as these images are, they add little to our scientific knowledge of the problem.

Exaggeration Does a Disservice

It's difficult to cover this problem without being accused of anti-environmentalism. That isn't the case—plastic contamination in the oceans simply shouldn't be there, and there's no doubt that this is a problem that needs to be taken seriously. However, by attempting to spin tales of plastic "continents," environmentalists risk shooting themselves in the foot. People have little patience for such easily debunked claims, and there's a real danger of being the boy who cried wolf.

What we need aren't publicity stunts and travel blogs, but comprehensive research to understand the true extent of the problem, and what we can do about it. Feeding myths to the media doesn't aid this understanding, it simply misleads the public, and ultimately undermines those of us trying to pitch a rational environmentalist message.

You don't need to invent an eighth continent to persuade people that plastic in the oceans is a problem.

EVALUATING THE AUTHOR'S ARGUMENTS:

Martin Robbins quotes from several sources to support the points he makes in his essay. Make a list of all the people he quotes, including their credentials and the nature of their comments. Then pick the quote you found most persuasive. Why did you choose it? What did it lend to Robbins's argument?

Noise Pollution Is a Serious Threat to Marine Mammals

"Undersea noise from human activities . . . poses a potentially major threat to marine animals of many kinds worldwide."

International Fund for Animal Welfare

The International Fund for Animal Welfare (IFAW) works to protect animals from abuse, cruelty, and harm. In the following viewpoint it argues that marine mammals are threatened by noise pollution. IFAW contends that today's oceans are very loud—noise comes from commercial shipping freighters, seismic exploration, sonar technology, and underwater construction. The noise from these activities is increasingly making it hard for dolphins, whales, seals, and other marine animals to hear. IFAW says hearing is critical for these animals, who rely on sound to help them find food, mates, and breeding grounds and to avoid harm. IFAW warns that if the oceans are too noisy, these populations will have trouble mating, feeding, and communicating with each other. The organization concludes that efforts must be made to reduce underwater noise pollution in order to protect marine species from harm.

In 1956 legendary marine explorer Jacques Cousteau described the oceans as "The Silent World" in his film documentary of that name. This description was more romantic than factual: the ocean depths have always been alive with sound, from the breaking of waves to the voices of marine animals beyond count. Today, however, Cousteau's silence is noisier than it has ever been before. In recent decades undersea noise from human activities has increased dramatically. This increase is set to continue and, unless tackled, poses a potentially major threat to marine animals of many kinds worldwide.

Commercial shipping, seismic exploration, sonar technology, marine construction, dredging and seabed drilling have all benefited humanity. But collectively they have now raised background ocean noise to potentially threatening levels. Shipping is the biggest single contributor, through its propeller and engine noise. Between 1965 and 2003 the world's commercial fleet doubled in size. According to one study, ship noise pollution in the Pacific has doubled every decade for the past 40 years. This alarming trend is likely to accelerate; the fleet is forecast to at least double again by 2025.

Noisy Oceans Threaten Wildlife

For people, even relatively low level noise can cause psychological and physical stress, adversely affecting blood pressure, heart rate and cardiac output. But people can usually move away from noise—for ocean creatures escape is often impossible. Sound travels nearly five times faster in water than in air and can invade tens of thousands of square kilometres in seconds.

Moreover, marine animals have developed sensitive hearing and complex sound-making repertoires, such as echolocation, with which to navigate, communicate, detect mates or rivals, maintain group cohesion and find food in their largely dark environment. Cetaceans— whales, dolphins and porpoises—have particularly sensitive hearing and their reliance on sound is almost total.

Man-made noise has begun to interfere with and even drown out these crucial sound-based systems. The mighty blue whale once communicated across entire oceans, but no longer; noise pollution has reduced its acoustic range by nine-tenths. Such effects must inevitably pose serious questions about these animals' continued ability to find mates and food in the vastness of the oceans.

Ocean noise pollution is also being linked with behavioural changes that have been seen in marine animals around the world, including the abandonment of preferred habitat, alterations in surfacing and

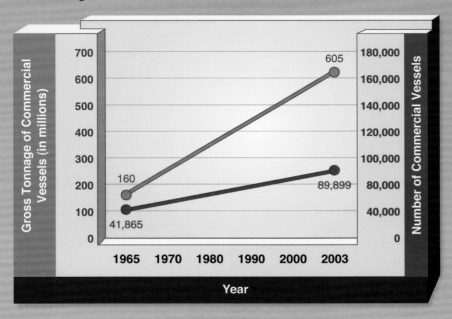

The Number of Ships Has Increased Exponentially

There has been a significant increase in shipping traffic since the 1960s. This traffic generates noise, which could harm marine mammals.

Taken from: International Fund for Animal Welfare, "Ocean Noise: Turn it Down," June 2008.

diving patterns and in the types, timing and volume of calls. At least some cetaceans are known to have changed their calls as they struggle to make themselves heard. Ocean noise pollution may also be behind incidences in which marine animals have abandoned vital activities, such as feeding. It may even be causing fatalities: high intensity military sonar is implicated in the deaths of beaked whales and mass strandings of cetaceans around the world.

So the Silent World is now a noisy place indeed and that noise is increasing. Neither the extent of the detrimental effects of this insidious form of pollution nor its consequences for marine animals are yet clear. Unless the international community takes action to tackle ocean noise pollution, however, we are likely to discover only too late the damage we are causing. . . .

The Importance of Sound to Marine Life

Sunlight fades rapidly beneath the surface of the oceans. Thirty metres down most colours have been absorbed, by 200 metres light is all but gone. Below 1,000 metres the ocean is a place of complete darkness. In the underwater world sound is king.

Marine mammals use sound to navigate and to detect predators and prey. It is essential for communication in order to attract mates, announce location and territory, to establish dominance and maintain group cohesion and social interaction. The toothed whales or odontocetes—which include dolphins, porpoises, beaked whales, sperm whales and killer whales—use echolocation to obtain environmental information such as water depth, the location of food and the distance of objects.

This means that marine mammals need to make and use sound continually. The sounds they make vary greatly, however. Toothed whales make a variety of clicks and whistles. Baleen whales emit tonal moans but also knocks, pulses, thumps and trumpet-like sounds. Humpback and bowhead whales famously make extended "songs" in their breeding grounds. Meanwhile the pinnipeds—seals, sea lions and walruses—also make a wide range of sounds. Marine mammals' calls occupy a huge variety of frequencies ranging from the high pitched 120–150 kHz echolocation clicks of the harbour porpoise to the ultra low frequency 10–15 second booms of the blue whale, which can be lower than 20 Hz and travel many hundreds of kilome-

Volunteers in New Zealand help rescue eighty-five whales found stranded on a beach. Human-made sounds interfere with marine mammals' sensitive hearing, on which they rely for navigation, finding food, and listening to communication from others of their species.

tres. Both these animals' calls are beyond the range of human hearing but those of many of the world's other marine mammal species are audible to us.

Hearing Is a Critical Sense

To detect these sounds over vast ocean areas marine mammals have developed acute hearing, which is attuned to broader frequency ranges than are common in land mammals. Darlene R. Ketten, a senior scientist at Woods Hole Oceanographic Institution, maintains: "Hearing is arguably their premier sensory system—it is obvious from their level of ear and neural auditory centre development alone. Dolphins and whales devote three-fold more neurons to hearing than any other animal. The temporal lobes, which control higher auditory processing, dominate their brain and they may have more complex auditory and signal processing capabilities than most mammals."

While it appears that the mechanisms of hearing damage are similar in both land and marine mammals, currently there is relatively little information on how the latter respond to intense sound.

Audiograms—records of hearing ability that can be used to measure hearing loss—exist only for about 20 marine mammal species, all of which are toothed whales and pinnipeds that were tested in captivity. This means that there is no direct behavioural or physiological hearing data for almost 80 per cent of marine mammals. . . .

Too Much Noise Can Kill

The effects of man-made ocean noise on marine mammals depend on a variety of factors, including the nature of the sound, its frequency, intensity and duration and the type of animal concerned. There is considerable uncertainty over the effects of noise exposure on marine animals yet as evidence has accumulated the issue has received increasing attention from scientists and international bodies.

Suggestions that man-made ocean noise poses problems for marine animals first began to emerge in the 1970s. Since then scientific studies have established that some man-made sounds can injure some marine mammals and fish, disrupt or mask crucial sounds on which they depend and also cause behavioural changes. On occasion ocean noise has even been shown to kill, with well-documented cases of fatal mass strandings of cetaceans following the use of military sonar in Greece, Madeira, Hawaii and coastal USA, the Virgin Islands, Spain, the Canary Islands and the Bahamas. In a 2001 joint report with the National Marine Fisheries Service the US Navy accepted for the first time that sonar used by its ships was the most plausible cause of the beaching of 16 whales in the Bahamas in March 2000.

In 2004 the Scientific Committee of the International Whaling Commission (IWC), consisting of more than 100 scientists from many countries, agreed unanimously that there was "compelling evidence implicating military sonar as a direct impact on beaked whales in particular." They also advised that "evidence of increased sounds from other sources, including ships and seismic activities, were cause for serious concern."

Noise Displaces Animals and Masks Important Sounds

There are three main areas of concern about the potential effects of ocean noise pollution on marine animals:

1. That intense noise exposure may cause death or physical injury, even at low levels for some vulnerable species (including temporary or permanent hearing loss), as well as increased stress leading to detrimental consequences for animals' immune systems and reproductive health.
2. That man-made ocean noise may mask sounds that are vital to marine animals, such as those indicating the existence and location of prey, predators and mates, as well as navigational information.
3. That noise exposure may cause behavioural changes ranging from minor to severe. Noise pollution may interfere with biologically important activities, including breeding and calving and with the use of historical migration routes and feeding grounds.

A number of scientific studies have shown the effects of ocean noise pollution on behaviour:

- Bottlenose dolphins and pilot, sperm and killer whales have altered their call rates when exposed to low and mid-frequency noise sources.
- When gray whales were exposed to industrial sounds they left one of their breeding sites for more than five years, returning only several years after the noise stopped.
- Loud acoustic harassment can displace killer whales and harbour porpoises over seasons or years.

A Threat to Whole Populations

Some animals may remain near noise sources but this does not mean that they are not affected by them: they might remain to feed or mate even to the point of damaging their hearing.

Scientists reported that humpback whales exposed to explosions associated with construction off Newfoundland showed little behavioural reaction to the noise yet were subsequently much more likely to become fatally entangled in fishing nets. They concluded this "may have occurred because of sensitivity threshold shifts or damaged hearing. This suggests that caution is needed in interpreting lack of visible reactions to sounds as an indication that whales are not affected, or harmed, by an intensive acoustic stimulus."

Few studies have been able to quantify the long-term effects on marine mammals of exposure to man-made ocean noise. Whilst brief or single acute exposures to sound may injure individual animals, long-term continuous noise from multiple sources is potentially more serious as it could cause changes to behaviour and habitat use that could affect whole populations. The consequences for marine mammals of continuous exposure to increasing background noise levels in the oceans are unknown.

EVALUATING THE AUTHOR'S ARGUMENTS:

The International Fund for Animal Welfare says that ocean noise must be reduced in order to protect marine mammals from harm, even death. Given what you know on this topic, what suggestions would you make for reducing the amount of underwater noise pollution? What activities, programs, or inventions might help solve this problem? Flesh out your solution over two to three paragraphs.

Chapter 3

How Should Oceans Be Protected?

The April 21, 2010, Deepwater Horizon Oil Rig explosion and the subsequent ecological disaster in the Gulf of Mexico have highlighted the need to protect the world's oceans.

Viewpoint

1

Deepwater Oil Drilling Should Be Banned

Matthew Daly

"'There is no safe way to drill for oil and gas, and we don't want to see another spill.'"

In the following viewpoint Matthew Daly discusses President Barack Obama's ban on deepwater oil drilling in the Gulf of Mexico. While the oil and gas industry has concerns over Obama's ban, Daly says environmental groups are cheering his decision. Jacqueline Savitz of the advocacy group Oceana claims that there is no safe way to drill for oil without risking another spill and that having such a ban will help protect the environment. Daly is a reporter for the Associated Press, covering environmental and energy issues.

AS YOU READ, CONSIDER THE FOLLOWING QUESTIONS:
1. As stated in the article, what was the most important lesson the British Petroleum (BP) oil spill taught officials?
2. Already-planned oil lease sales in the Gulf of Mexico will be delayed until when?
3. What does Florida governor Charlie Crist call the BP oil spill?

B P's [British Petroleum's] oil well in the Gulf of Mexico is dead, but the political fallout is very much alive.

The [Barack] Obama administration said it won't open up new areas of the eastern Gulf and Atlantic seaboard to drilling, reversing a decision to hunt for oil and gas that the president himself announced three weeks before the largest offshore oil spill in U.S. history.

"We are adjusting our strategy," Interior Secretary Ken Salazar said Wednesday.

Salazar said the BP spill taught officials a number of lessons, "most importantly that we need to proceed with caution."

The politics of the decision were clear. The ban satisfies environmental interests and Democratic lawmakers along both coasts, particularly in Florida, a crucial 2012 swing state where the drilling proposal was unpopular.

The Concern Over a Ban

But the oil and gas industry and many Republicans said the Obama administration was stifling domestic oil production and contradicting the will of recession-weary voters eager for new jobs.

This dead sea turtle in Louisiana is a victim of a deepwater oil spill. One reason for President Barack Obama's controversial ban on deepwater drilling was the devastating effects of oil spills on the environment.

Rep. Doc Hastings, R-Wash., said Obama's plan would lock up vast portions of America's offshore energy resources, costing jobs and inflicting long-term economic harm. Hastings, who takes over next month as chairman of the House Natural Resources panel, said the BP spill shouldn't disrupt plans to develop U.S. oil and gas resources.

Louisiana Gov. Bobby Jindal, a Republican who has criticized the Obama administration's response to the spill and its five-month deepwater drilling moratorium, expressed deep disappointment. "This makes us even more dependent on foreign countries for our energy," he said.

And Sen. Mark Warner, D-Va., who supports offshore drilling, was preparing to work with GOP Gov. Robert McDonnell and other officials to re-examine the decision, especially as it applies to Virginia, said Kevin Hall, a Warner spokesman.

The announcement reverses a March [2010] plan that would have authorized officials to explore the potential for drilling from Delaware to central Florida, plus the northern waters of Alaska. The new approach allows drilling in Alaska, but officials said they will move cautiously before approving any leases. The focus instead will be on areas with active leases in the central and western Gulf of Mexico and off the coast of Alaska.

Under the revised plan, the Interior Department will not propose any new oil drilling in the Atlantic Ocean and eastern Gulf for at least the next seven years. Already planned lease sales in the Gulf of Mexico will be delayed until late 2011 or early 2012, Salazar said.

The new plan does not affect the Pacific seaboard, which will remain off-limits to drilling in federal waters.

Support for a Drilling Ban

Environmental groups cheered the decision. They say oil and gas reserves off the Atlantic Coast are not worth the risk to commercial fishing and

When Deepwater Drilling Goes Wrong

The 2010 British Petroleum oil spill was the largest accidental oil spill in petroleum history. An explosion aboard an oil rig killed eleven people and spread millions of barrels of oil throughout the Gulf of Mexico.

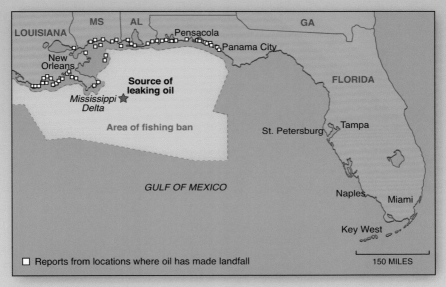

☐ Reports from locations where oil has made landfall   150 MILES

Government estimate of oil spilled in the Gulf of Mexico through August 2, 2010: 4.1 million barrels of oil

Where the oil has gone:

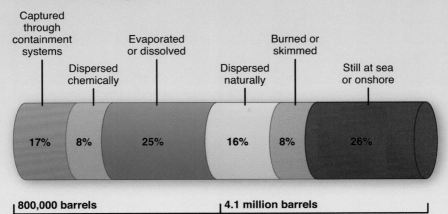

Captured through containment systems — 17%
Dispersed chemically — 8%
Evaporated or dissolved — 25%
Dispersed naturally — 16%
Burned or skimmed — 8%
Still at sea or onshore — 26%

800,000 barrels   4.1 million barrels

tourism destinations such as Virginia Beach and the Chesapeake Bay. According to government estimates, reserves off Virginia, North and South Carolina, Georgia and north Florida amount to about three months of supply at current U.S. consumption rates.

"There is no safe way to drill for oil and gas, and we don't want to see another spill," said Jacqueline Savitz at the advocacy group Oceana.

Sen. Robert Menendez, D-N.J., who championed a ban on East Coast drilling, called it a victory for his state's coastline. "Auctioning off the Jersey shore to oil companies would do nothing to reduce prices at the pump, but it would put our multibillion-dollar tourism and fishing industries at risk," he said.

Exxon Mobil executive Kenneth Cohen countered that the government decision ignored the industry's improving safety performance. He said the Gulf spill "resulted from practices far outside industry norms."

Florida Gov. Charlie Crist, a Republican turned independent, once considered opening state waters to drilling, but changed his mind after the BP spill. He wasn't surprised by the administration's reversal.

"If that's not a wake-up call, I don't know what would be," Crist said.

EVALUATING THE AUTHOR'S ARGUMENTS:

Matthew Daly lays out the pros and cons of why deepwater drilling should be banned. Make a list of at least two pros and two cons. Then, state whether you think deepwater drilling should be banned and cite at least one piece of evidence that swayed you.

Deepwater Oil Drilling Should Not Be Banned

Jane Wardell and Jennifer Quinn

"Hornbeck Offshore Services of Covington, Louisiana, ... claims the government arbitrarily imposed the moratorium without any proof that the operations posed a threat."

Jane Wardell and Jennifer Quinn are writers for the Associated Press. In the following viewpoint Wardell and Quinn explain the oil industry's belief that deepwater oil drilling should not be banned. The oil executives believe that the ban would cripple the world's energy supplies. Although the process of deepwater drilling is seen as risky and expensive, the industry believes it is a necessity in a world where oil supplies in shallow water are running out. British Petroleum chief of staff Steve Westwell claims that the world needs the energy and oil that comes from deepwater drilling.

AS YOU READ, CONSIDER THE FOLLOWING QUESTIONS:
  1. For how long did President Barack Obama declare a morato-
     rium on deepwater drilling in the Gulf of Mexico?
  2. Who called the deepwater ban an "unnecessary reaction" to the
     April 20 explosion?
  3. According to Hornbeck Offshore Services, what could
     Obama's moratorium cost Louisiana?

Oil executives sent a strong challenge to Barack Obama on Tuesday, warning at a major oil conference that the American president's ban on risky deepwater drilling would cripple world energy supplies.

As a BP [British Petroleum] executive standing in for embattled CEO Tony Hayward was heckled by protesters, other industry leaders used the gathering to rally around the British company, arguing that eliminating deepsea rigs in the wake of the Gulf of Mexico oil spill was unsustainable.

BP's stock slid to a 13-year-low Tuesday in London, and the oil giant confirmed that Hayward was already in the process of handing over control of the Gulf oil spill to managing director Bob Dudley.

Obama slapped a six-month moratorium on deepwater drilling in the Gulf as part of his struggle to show that his administration is responding forcefully to the disaster. The decision halted the approval of any new permits for deepwater drilling and suspended drilling at 33 existing exploratory wells in the Gulf.

A federal judge in New Orleans blocked the moratorium on Tuesday, and the White House promised an immediate appeal.

The ban reflects growing unease about oil companies seeking to drill farther out to sea and deeper than ever before. The process is

FAST FACT

Because oil production from fields lying in shallow waters in the Gulf of Mexico peaked in the 1990s, 80 percent of the oil reserves that remain in the gulf are either in deep or very deep water, according to Boston University professor of geography and environment Cutler Cleveland.

expensive, risky and largely uncharted—but the industry argues it is also necessary in a world where land and shallow water oil supplies are running out.

Unnecessary Reaction

Transocean Ltd. president and CEO Steven Newman, owner of the Deepwater Horizon rig where an April 20 explosion killed 11 workers

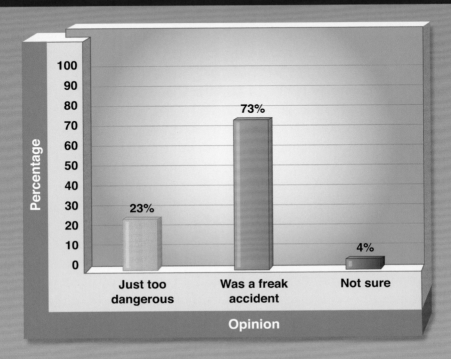

Americans Still Favor Offshore Drilling

Even after the catastrophic British Petroleum (BP) oil spill of 2010, the majority of Americans think deepwater oil drilling should be allowed to continue.

Question:
Do you think the BP spill proves offshore drilling is just too dangerous and should be banned in US waters, or was this a freak accident and offshore drilling can be made safer and not be banned?

Taken from: Bloomberg/Selzer & Co., July 9–12, 2010.

Although the Deepwater Horizon oil spill devastated his state's coastline, Louisiana governor Bobby Jindal, pictured, believes deepwater oil drilling should not be banned.

and set off the worst oil spill in U.S. history, called the deepwater ban an unnecessary overreaction.

"There are things the administration could implement today that would allow the industry to go back to work tomorrow without an arbitrary six-month time limit," Newman told reporters on the sidelines of the conference in the British capital. "Obviously we are concerned."

Chevron executive Jay Pryor said the U.S. government's move will "constrain supplies for world energy."

"It would also be a step back for energy security," Pryor, global vice president for business development at the U.S. company, told delegates at the World National Oil Companies Congress.

The moratorium was challenged in court by an oil services company, Hornbeck Offshore Services of Covington, Louisiana, which claims the government arbitrarily imposed the moratorium without any proof that the operations posed a threat. A federal judge in New Orleans, Judge Martin Feldman, on Tuesday lifted the moratorium.

Hornbeck, which ferries people and supplies to offshore rigs, says the moratorium could cost Louisiana thousands of jobs and millions of dollars in lost wages.

In addition to the Gulf, there are more than 20 offshore rigs in Britain's North Sea, although they do not operate in waters as deep as the Gulf. Brazil, which sits on the world's potentially largest deepwater oil beds, has no deepwater rigs yet but plans to build 28 rigs in the coming years.

BP chief of staff Steve Westwell, who was heckled as he stood in for Hayward, said "regulators around the world will obviously want to know what happened" to cause the blown-out well in the Gulf and will change their procedures accordingly.

"The world does need the oil and the energy that is going to have to come from deepwater production going forward," Westwell said. "Therefore, the regulatory framework must still enable that to be a viable commercial position." . . .

BP signed an exploration and production deal with Libya's National Oil Co.—worth at least $900 million—in June 2007, sending the company back into Libya for the first time in more than 30 years. Libya's proven oil reserves are the ninth largest in the world, while vast areas remain unexplored for new deposits.

Libya has said it plans to start deepwater drilling in the Mediterranean "pretty soon."

Some believe the oil industry may be crying wolf. Many analysts say the continued strength of oil prices, which have mostly fluctuated between $70 and $85 over the past months, can be attributed to excessive speculation in the futures market. In reality, there has been a slow recovery of oil demand since the global credit squeeze and there are huge stockpiles of crude and refined products in the United States. . . .

EVALUATING THE AUTHORS' ARGUMENTS:

Jane Wardell and Jennifer Quinn use quotations from a major oil conference to make the argument that deepwater oil drilling should not be banned. Do these quotations strengthen their argument? Would quotations from other experts help the authors further persuade the reader?

Protecting Fish Populations Will Solve the Overfishing Crisis

John Hocevar and Jeremy Jackson

"Across our oceans, fish have nowhere to find refuge and replenish their population— which is why we need to . . . establish a network of no-take marine reserves."

In the following viewpoint John Hocevar and Jeremy Jackson argue that fish are being taken out of the ocean at an alarmingly destructive rate. If this level of overfishing continues, they warn, fish stocks will crash, taking a valuable food source and lucrative industry with them, as well as damaging the marine ecology. For these reasons, the authors say, fishers need to be prevented from overfishing the sea, and marine preserves need to be established to protect fish populations and thus reverse the crisis caused by overfishing.

Hocevar is a marine biologist and the director of Greenpeace's Defending Our Oceans campaign. Jackson is a professor of oceanography at the Scripps Institution of Oceanography in San Diego, California.

AS YOU READ, CONSIDER THE FOLLOWING QUESTIONS:
  1. According to the authors, what has happened to the Alaska pollock population since 2003?
  2. What is the status of Alaska's four pollock fisheries, according to Hocevar and Jackson?
  3. How many people do the authors say lost their jobs when an Atlantic cod fishery was closed in 1994?

I f you like seafood, you've probably eaten Alaska pollock, the tender white fish used in most frozen fish sticks, McDonald's Filet-O-Fish sandwiches, and the imitation crab meat found in California rolls. But the pollock—the world's largest food fishery—is on the verge of collapse.

Fisheries Are Under Enormous Strain

The most recent data from the National Marine Fisheries Service show the pollock population approaching the lowest level ever recorded; since 2003, the population has declined from 8.5 million tons to 3 million tons. That's bad news for fish eaters and fishermen alike, and really bad news for Alaska's extraordinary ocean ecosystem.

> **FAST FACT**
>
> The main threats to critically endangered leatherback sea turtles include being unintentionally caught by fishing gear, habitat destruction, and the harvest of eggs and adults on nesting beaches, according to a 2010 article by the National Oceanic and Atmospheric Administration.

Even as the pollock—and the wildlife that rely on them—have declined, the government has allowed overfishing to continue. Incredibly, these steep declines do not even meet the government's definition of overfished.

As a result, two of Alaska's four pollock fisheries have been closed and a third is just a fraction of its former size. Until recently, though, the strength of the Bering Sea pollock stock was sufficient to support a

billion dollar industry and earn a "sustainable" rating from the Marine Stewardship Council.

Repeating Mistakes of the Past

But like economics, fisheries management involves too many variables and too much uncertainty for anyone to make precise predictions. And, as with the economy, when large amounts of money are at stake, managers tend to downplay that uncertainty and hope for the best.

That's exactly what happened to the Atlantic cod, the pollock's close relative, and the previous holder of the title "world's biggest food fishery." For years, the Atlantic fish industry refused to heed the warning signs that cod was in serious trouble and tighter regulation was needed.

When policy makers did finally act, in 1992, it was too late—and the fishery crashed to less than one percent of its former level. By 1994, the fishery, which had been active since at least the beginning of the 16th century, had to be closed. Suddenly, more than 40,000 people were out of work and the industry went begging to the government for a multi-billion dollar bailout.

Today, the North Pacific Fisheries Council seems to be repeating the cod tragedy.

Saving the Fishing Industry from Itself

Despite the warning signs, including several years of low juvenile survivorship, the Council continues to allow trawlers to kill the fish that lay the golden eggs. Each winter, factory trawlers brave the stormy Bering Sea to target spawning pollock, killing huge numbers of pregnant females before they release their eggs, or roe. The roe fishery is lucrative but ecologically dangerous even in the best of times. At a time when the pollock population needs all the offspring it can produce—and global warming seems to be putting additional stress on the fishery—it's just reckless. The Council members (mostly representatives of the fishing industry) persist in saying that we can trust the industry to police itself—and are increasingly sounding like the Alan Greenspans [former chair of the Federal Reserve System] of the sea.

It's still theoretically possible that environmental conditions will allow for a season of epic pollock reproduction that will begin to

An Alaskan fishing boat crew loads pollock into their boat's hold. Overfishing has caused two of the state's four pollock fisheries to close.

re-build the stock. If we continue with business as usual, though, it's more likely that the fishery will collapse, with devastating consequences for the wildlife and people of Alaska.

The next year or two may be our last chance to save the fishing industry from itself. The key will be in taking action before things reach the point of no return, as appears to have happened with cod. Most immediately, the pollock catch needs to be cut significantly, and the roe fishery should be suspended.

Drastic Measures Are Necessary—and Fast

Many of the measures necessary to save the pollock fishery are just as needed in other fisheries around the country that are also reeling from overfishing. Across our oceans, fish have nowhere to find refuge and replenish their population—which is why we need to move quickly to establish a network of no-take marine reserves.

Until we move from simply managing fisheries in a vacuum to protecting the ecosystems that sustain them, fisheries managers will continue to be surprised by one economic and ecological disaster after another—and taxpayers could find themselves on the hook for yet another multi-billion dollar bailout.

EVALUATING THE AUTHORS' ARGUMENTS:

In this viewpoint John Hocevar and Jeremy Jackson argue that overfishing needs to be prevented so that the ecological crisis it has caused can be reversed. But Don Hansen, author of the following viewpoint, argues that there is no overfishing crisis. After reading both viewpoints, do you think a fishing crisis exists or not? Identify at least two key pieces of evidence that swayed you.

The Overfishing Crisis Is a Myth

Don Hansen

"The fisheries crisis that protected areas are supposed to solve simply doesn't exist."

Don Hansen is the former chair of the Pacific Fishery Management Council. In the following viewpoint he argues that establishing marine preserves in which fishing is not allowed is unnecessary because there is no overfishing crisis, at least on the western coast of the United States. All of the fisheries there are healthy and thriving, he says. Therefore, not only do these areas not need protection, but such protection comes at a steep price: the jobs of fishers and millions of dollars of taxpayer funds. Hansen concludes that it is foolish to adopt harsh measures to regulate a crisis that does not exist. He recommends that more balanced measures be adopted to ensure that fishers have jobs and that fish are reasonably conserved.

AS YOU READ, CONSIDER THE FOLLOWING QUESTIONS:

1. What is the Marine Life Protection Act and why does the author disagree with it?
2. Of the ninety fish stocks that would receive protection, how many does Hansen say have actually been designated as being overfished?
3. What, according to the author, are greater threats to oceans than overfishing?

For years, California's citizens have been told that the state's marine fisheries are being overfished and are in a state of rapid decline and that the only way to solve this crisis is to stop people from fishing.

[Since 2004], under the Marine Life Protection Act, California has been establishing a system of marine protected areas along California's coast to address the "fisheries crisis." The state is doing this largely by creating draconian no-fishing zones that prevent recreational anglers and their families from going out for a day's fishing. The process, however, is costing millions of dollars to implement and is having serious financial impacts on coastal communities which depend on recreational fishing. All to address a fishing crisis that simply doesn't exist.

There Is No Overfishing Crisis

While there are examples of overfishing and declining fish stocks in oceans around the world, such is not the case off the coasts of California, Oregon and Washington. The fisheries crisis that protected areas are supposed to solve simply doesn't exist. In these three states, there is not one marine fisheries stock currently experiencing overfishing, and the few stocks still experiencing stress can be found in abundance due to the strict management and rebuilding plans established more than 20 years ago. For example, of the more than 90 groundfish stocks most likely to benefit from a marine protected area, only nine have been designated as overfished. Two of those stocks have been declared rebuilt in the past five years, and the remaining seven are all under strict rebuilding plans. In addition to these fishery management measures, prime marine habitat is being protected via a ban on destructive commercial fishing practices such as bottom trawling. California's marine fisheries and ocean resource management program is working.

FAST FACT

According to the Fisheries and Aquaculture Organization of the United Nations, over 500 million people in developing countries depend on fishing for their livelihoods.

In addition, in a recent article in *Science* magazine, professors Boris Worm of Canada's Dalhousie University and Ray Hilborn of the University of Washington state that California's fisheries are flourishing. The article proves that California can have robust fishing opportunities and healthy ocean ecosystems at the same time.

Reasons for Protection No Longer Apply

In fact, the arguments that were used to pass the protection act more than a decade ago simply no longer hold true. Terrestrial pollution is having a far more significant impact on our oceans. Climate change and ocean acidification, global problems regularly associated with our oceans' decline, have nothing to do with recreational fishing. Marine protected areas will not solve these problems nor be an effective tool in mitigating their impact.

Designating protected areas in state waters will not cure the ocean of what ails it. The key to solving our oceans' problems is to find a balance between extraction and conservation. This can be found in Proposal 2, one of the three currently [in 2009] before the Marine Life

Fishing boats lie moored in San Francisco Bay. The author contends that establishing marine preserves in which fishing is not allowed is unnecessary and threatens jobs.

Protection Act Blue Ribbon Task Force. It is undoubtedly the best way to effectively manage California's marine resources for human use while maintaining our fish stocks. California's policy makers need to ask themselves—can our state afford to fix a crisis that doesn't exist? The hype and noise about recreational overfishing is, quite simply, overblown.

Achieving the Right Balance

Crafted by anglers, commercial fishermen, city officials, harbor masters, the Department of Defense and wastewater representatives, Proposal 2 protects 16 percent of southern California's ocean environment and has tremendous conservation value. It protects many of the most biologically productive and diverse marine habitats in the state, including lush kelp forests, rugged reef systems, submarine canyons, intertidal coastal stretches, surf grass beds, pinniped [seal and sea lion] rookeries, avian [bird] roosting sites, estuaries and tidal flats.

Proposal 2 is an integrated proposal, maximizing conservation goals while at the same time minimizing the impact on those who enjoy the sport of fishing as well as those who depend on fishing for their livelihood. More importantly, it provides significant additional protection for ocean resources, which currently are healthy and sustainable.

EVALUATING THE AUTHOR'S ARGUMENTS:

Don Hansen uses facts, statistics, examples, and reasoning to make his argument that an overfishing crisis does not exist. He does not, however, use any quotations to support his point. If you were to rewrite this article and insert quotations, what authorities might you quote? Where would you place the quotations, and why?

Facts About Oceans

Editor's note: These facts can be used in reports to add credibility when making important points or claims.

Facts About the World's Oceans

- Oceans make up about 140 million square miles, or about 70 percent, of the earth's surface area.
- The average depth of the ocean is more than 2.5 miles.
- The lowest point on earth is -36,198 feet, in the Mariana Trench in the western Pacific Ocean.
- The average temperature of the oceans is about 39°F.
- The earth's waters are divided into five major oceans: Pacific, Atlantic, Indian, Antarctic (or Southern), and Arctic.
- Although scientists have traditionally divided the planet's ocean water into five separate oceans, these waters are frequently viewed by scientists as being one big, interconnected waterway, sometimes called the World Ocean.
- The oceans contain over 80 percent of all life on earth.
- Oceans are a part of the earth's water cycle; most of the water in rain comes from the evaporation of ocean water.
- More than 97 percent of all the water on earth is contained in the oceans.
- One gallon of seawater contains about one-half cup of salt.
- Australia's Great Barrier Reef, measuring 1,243 miles, is the largest living structure on earth and can be seen from the moon.

Facts About Oceans and Global Warming

- Scientists around the world gather information about the oceans using a robotic probe called an Argo float. There are more than thirty-two thousand Argo floats in the world's oceans; these collect data such as water temperatures and transmit the data to scientists via satellite.

- The top 10 feet of the ocean hold as much heat as the earth's entire atmosphere.
- According to a 2010 report in the journal *Nature*, the global phytoplankton population has decreased by roughly 40 percent since 1950, largely due to increased surface temperatures in the seas.
- According to a 2009 report in *National Geographic*, if global warming continues unchecked, oxygen-poor "dead zones" could encompass more than one-fifth of the world's oceans by 2100, affecting marine life for thousands of years to come.

Facts About Oceans and Fish Stocks

- According to the National Oceanic and Atmospheric Administration, there are at least twenty thousand different species of fish living in the oceans.
- According to the International Food Policy Research Institute, global fish consumption more than doubled from 1973 to 1997, primarily because of population growth in poor countries and the increased demands for fish there.
- The loss of large, predatory sharks may lead to an imbalance in the ecosystem; according to a 2000 study published in the *Journal of Marine Science*, the removal of tiger sharks in waters near the Hawaiian Islands caused the number of reef shark, sea turtle, and seabirds to increase, while the number of tuna and jack decreased.
- According to a 2006 study published in the journal *Ecology Letters*, an estimated 26 million to 73 million sharks were killed worldwide in 2000 to supply the global demand for shark fins, popular in Chinese cuisine such as shark fin soup.
- According to the International Shark Attack File, run by the Florida Museum of Natural History, the odds of dying in a shark attack, or of being attacked by a shark at all, are very slim:
  - A person's chance of being attacked by a shark is 1 in 11.5 million.
  - It is more likely that someone will get struck by lightning, get eaten by an alligator, or die in a boating accident than be attacked by a shark or die from a shark attack.
  - Between 1990 and 2008, there were 14,379 fatalities resulting from bike accidents. In this same time, there were only 13 shark attacks.

- Hunting accident fatalities also greatly outnumber shark fatalities: In the United States and Canada from 2000 to 2007, there were 4,495 deaths from hunting accidents and only 7 from shark attacks.
- On average, there are only about 65 shark attacks worldwide each year, and just a few of these are fatal.

Facts About Pollution in the Oceans

- Eighty percent of all pollution in the ocean comes from land-based activities.
- A major contributor to pollution from ocean-based activities is cruise ships; an average-sized cruise ship produces around 1 million gallons of wastewater in a week.
- Plastic waste kills up to 1 million seabirds, 100,000 sea mammals, and countless fish each year.
- In 1997 scientists discovered a floating mass of trash in the ocean between California and Hawaii; called the Great Pacific Garbage Patch, it is estimated to be at least as big as Texas.
- In 2010 scientists discovered a second garbage patch; called the North Atlantic Garbage Patch, it is believed to be as big as the patch in the Pacific Ocean.
- Birds and other wildlife mistake bits of plastic and other trash in the ocean for food and eat it; the trash does not digest and blocks the animals' digestive systems, causing the animals to starve to death.
- Sea turtles, dolphins, and other marine animals have been trapped by items such as plastic fishing nets and have been injured or even killed when becoming entangled in these items.

Americans' Opinions About Oceans

According to an ABC News/*Washington Post*/Stanford University poll conducted April 5–10, 2007:

- When asked how much the depletion of fish stocks through overfishing concerned them, 38 percent of those surveyed said it concerned them a great deal, 25 percent said it concerned them a good amount, 23 percent said it concerned them just some, and 13 percent said it concerned them hardly any or not at all.
- When asked how much pollution of the oceans concerned them, 52 percent said it concerned them a great deal, 25 percent said

it concerned them a good amount, 16 percent said it concerned them just some, and 6 percent said it concerned them hardly any or not at all.

- When asked how much rising sea levels due to global warming concerned them, 35 percent said it concerned them a great deal, 23 percent said it concerned them a good amount, 22 percent said it concerned them just some, and 18 percent said it concerned them hardly any or not at all.
- Fifty-one percent of those surveyed said they thought the federal government should do more to regulate commercial fishing in US waters, and 3 percent said the government should do less.
- Forty-one percent said they thought the federal government should leave the rules that regulate commercial fishing in US waters as they are.

Organizations to Contact

The editors have compiled the following list of organizations concerned with the issues debated in this book. The descriptions are derived from materials provided by the organizations. All have publications or information available for interested readers. The list was compiled on the date of publication of the present volume; the information provided here may change. Be aware that many organizations take several weeks or longer to respond to inquiries, so allow as much time as possible for the receipt of requested materials.

Antarctic and Southern Ocean Coalition (ASOC)
1630 Connecticut Ave. NW, 3rd Fl.
Washington, DC 20009
(202) 234-2480
fax: (202) 387-4823
e-mail: secretariat@asoc.org
website: www.asoc.org

The ASOC is a worldwide coalition of environmental nongovernmental organizations that works to ensure that the Antarctic continent, its surrounding islands, and the great Southern Ocean survive. The ASOC website contains links to reports and publications about Antarctic environmental issues, press releases, briefings, videos featuring wildlife, and the *Antarctica Blog.*

Coastal America Partnership
300 Seventh St. SW, Ste. 680
Washington, DC 20024
(202) 401-9928
fax: (202) 401-9821
e-mail: coastal.america@usda.gov
website: www.coastalamerica.gov

The Coastal America Partnership is a partnership of federal agencies, state and local governments, and private organizations dedicated to restoring and preserving coastal ecosystems and addressing critical environmental problems. Coastal America operates a number of Coastal Ecosystem Learning Centers, which include aquariums, marine science centers, and laboratories. Its website contains links to news articles, projects, and a student art contest, as well as a link to the newsletter *Coastal America Update* and other publications.

Greenpeace
702 H St. NW, Ste. 300
Washington, DC 20001
(202) 462-1177
e-mail: info@wdc.greenpeace.org
website: www.greenpeace.org

Greenpeace is a nongovernmental environmental activism organization that focuses on global issues, including many that affect the oceans, such as global warming, overfishing, and commercial whaling. Its website provides links to articles such as "Whale Defenders," "Bering Witness," and "Threats to Ocean Life," as well as a link to numerous reports concerning the health of oceans and marine life. A multimedia library of photos, slideshows, and videos is also available on the website.

International Union for Conservation of Nature (IUCN)
IUCN Conservation Centre
Rue Mauverney 28
Gland
1196
Switzerland
+41 (22) 999-0000
fax: +41 (22) 999-0002
e-mail: mail@iucn.org
website: www.iucn.org

The IUCN, the world's oldest and largest global environmental network, works to find solutions to the world's most pressing environmental and developmental challenges. It supports scientific research and brings governments, nongovernment organizations, United Nations agencies, corporations, and local communities together to develop and implement laws and policies.

National Ocean Industries Association (NOIA)

1120 G St. NW, Ste. 900
Washington, DC 20005
(202) 347-6900
fax: (202) 347-8650
e-mail: mkearns@noia.org
website: www.noia.org

The NOIA, founded in 1972, is dedicated to the development of offshore energy for the continued growth and security of the United States. It represents more than 205 member companies in the offshore energy industry, as well as companies that are pursuing offshore renewable and alternative energy opportunities. The association's website includes breaking news, links for press releases, and information on winners of the NOIA Safety in the Seas Award.

National Oceanic and Atmospheric Administration (NOAA)

1401 Constitution Ave. NW, Rm. 5128
Washington, DC 20230
e-mail: outreach@noaa.gov
website: www.noaa.gov

The NOAA is an agency within the US Department of Commerce that focuses on the conditions of the oceans and the atmosphere. Among other responsibilities, the NOAA charts the sky and the seas, guides the use and protection of ocean and coastal resources, and conducts research to aid in the understanding and protection of the environment.

Natural Resources Defense Council (NRDC)

40 W. Twentieth St.
New York, NY 10011
(212) 727-2700
fax: (212) 727-1773
e-mail: nrdcinfo@nrdc.org
website: www.nrdc.org

Founded in 1970, the NRDC actively works to curb global warming, to search for clean energy alternatives, to defend endangered wildlife and wild places, to prevent pollution, and to revive the world's oceans by ending overfishing, creating marine protected areas, and improving ocean governance.

The Nature Conservancy
Worldwide Office
4245 N. Fairfax Dr., Ste. 100
Arlington, VA 22203-1606
(703) 841-5300
website: www.nature.org

The Nature Conservancy works worldwide to protect ecologically important lands and waters on behalf of people and nature. Its website offers news releases, information about current initiatives, daily nature photos, a search engine that produces articles on oceans and marine conservation, and a link to the *Cool Green Science* blog.

Ocean Alliance
191 Weston Rd.
Lincoln, MA 01773
(781) 259-0423
fax: (781) 259-0288
e-mail: question@oceanalliance.org
website: www.oceanalliance.org

The Ocean Alliance is dedicated to the conservation of whales and their ocean habitat through research and education. It collects information on whales and ocean life, including toxicology, behavior, bioacoustics, and genetics. The alliance aims to reduce pollution, protect and preserve marine mammals and their environment, maintain human access to fish and other sea life, and benefit ocean and human health. Its website provides information on research, programs, press releases, blogs, and a link to the *Ocean Alliance* newsletter.

Sea Shepherd Conservation Society (SSCS)
PO Box 2616
Friday Harbor, WA 98250
(360) 370-5650
fax: (360) 370-5651
e-mail: info@seashepherd.org
website: www.seashepherd.org

The SSCS is an international nonprofit marine wildlife conservation organization. Its mission is to protect the habitat and wildlife in the world's oceans in order to safeguard the biodiversity of ocean ecosystems. The SSCS website contains links to news items, videos, information on current and past events, and campaigns to protect numerous species of sea life, including dolphins, seals, and whales. The society publishes a biannual newsletter, the *Sea Shepherd Log.*

Shark Alliance

c/o The Pew Charitable Trusts
901 E St. NW, 10th Fl.
Washington, DC 20004
(202) 552-2000
e-mail: info@sharkalliance.org
website: www.sharkalliance.org

The Shark Alliance is a global nonprofit coalition of nongovernmental organizations that work to restore and conserve shark populations by improving shark conservation policies. It is coordinated by the Pew Environment Group, the conservation arm of the Pew Charitable Trusts, a nongovernment organization that works to end overfishing in the world's oceans. The Shark Alliance website contains links to press releases, facts about sharks, information on events, and numerous publications concerning sharks throughout the world's oceans.

Sierra Club

85 Second St., 2nd Fl.
San Francisco, CA 94105
(415) 977-5500
fax: (415) 977-5799
e-mail: info@sierraclub.org
website: www.sierraclub.org

The Sierra Club is a grassroots environmental organization that works to protect communities, wild places, and the planet itself. Its website features news articles, links to several different blogs, an e-mail newsletter, and information about both local and international outings.

Surfrider Foundation

PO Box 6010
San Clemente, CA 92674-6010
(949) 492-8170
fax: (949) 492-8142

e-mail: info@surfrider.org
website: www.surfrider.org

The Surfrider Foundation is a nonprofit grassroots organization dedicated to the protection and enjoyment of the earth's oceans and beaches. The foundation includes over fifty thousand members and ninety chapters worldwide. Its website provides press releases, public service announcements, podcasts, samples from its *Music for Our Mother Ocean* CDs, and information on ways to volunteer. The foundation publishes the bimonthly magazine *Making Waves*.

US Environmental Protection Agency (EPA)
Ariel Rios Bldg.
1200 Pennsylvania Ave. NW
Washington, DC 20460
(202) 272-0167
website: www.epa.gov

The EPA's mission is to protect human health and the environment. Its website features news releases, research topics, information on laws and regulations, a science and technology section, and a search engine that brings up a wide variety of articles related to the oceans.

World Ocean Observatory
1 Oak St.
Boothbay Harbor, ME 04538
(800) 724-7245
e-mail: info@thew2o.net
website: www.thew2o.net

The World Ocean Observatory is a virtual educational enterprise that incorporates ocean information into exhibits, educational resources, public programs, and informational services and shares these resources through partnerships with existing museums, science centers, aquariums, libraries, and schools. Its website provides information on the oceans, upcoming events and exhibits, webcasts, downloadable segments from World Ocean Radio, and much more.

Worldwatch Institute
1776 Massachusetts Ave. NW
Washington, DC 20036-1904

(202) 452-1999
fax: (202) 296-7365
e-mail: worldwatch@worldwatch.org
website: www.worldwatch.org

Founded in 1974, the Worldwatch Institute is an independent environmental research organization that works to gather and disseminate data on climate change, resource degradation, and population growth. The institute's website features press releases, a variety of blogs, and a list of publications related to the health of the global environment, including its annual *State of the World* report.

For Further Reading

Books

Erle, Sylvia. *The World Is Blue: How Our Fate and the Ocean's Are One.* Washington, DC: National Geographic Society, 2010. The author, a scientist, uses personal stories to illustrate the current and future peril of the ocean and of ocean life.

Helvarg, David. *Blue Frontier: Dispatches from America's Ocean Wilderness.* San Francisco: Sierra Club, 2006. A comprehensive report on the state of America's oceans and the challenges they face today.

———. *50 Ways to Save the Ocean.* Makawao, HI: Inner Ocean, 2006. Presents simple, everyday actions that can help to protect and conserve the oceans, including which fish to eat and which to avoid, how and where to vacation, and ways to protect local water tables, reef environments, wetlands, and sanctuaries.

Knowlton, Nancy. *Citizens of the Sea: Wondrous Creatures from the Census of Marine Life.* Washington, DC: National Geographic Society, 2010. Filled with stunning full-color photographs of a wide variety of marine plants and animals, this book is also packed with informative tidbits about the oceans.

MacQuitty, Miranda. *Ocean.* London: DK, 2008. Part of the Eyewitness Books series, this volume provides an in-depth, comprehensive look at the oceans through informative text and plenty of interesting photographs.

National Geographic Society. *Ocean.* Washington, DC: National Geographic Society, 2010. Features numerous full-color photographs of the world's oceans, as well as a time line of great explorers and a section on the legacy of one of the world's best-known ocean explorers, Jacques Cousteau.

Periodicals and Internet Sources

Avery, Dennis T. "The Oceans Have Stopped Warming!," *Enter Stage Right,* March 31 2008. www.enterstageright.com/archive/articles/0408/0408globalwarmingoceans.htm.

BBC. "Whaling: The Japanese Position," January 15, 2008. http://news.bbc.co.uk/2/hi/asia-pacific/7153594.stm.

Bialik, Carl. "How Big Is That Widening Gyre of Floating Plastic?," *Wall Street Journal*, March 25, 2009. http://online.wsj.com/article/NA_WSJ_PUB:SB123793936249132307.html.

Biallo, David. "How Will Warmer Oceans Affect Sea Life?," *Scientific American*, August 25, 2009. www.scientificamerican.com/article.cfm?id=how-will-warmer-oceans-affect-sea-life.

Boljen, Steve. "Deep-Water Drilling Moratorium: Bad Economics," *Times of Trenton (NJ)*, July 24, 2010. www.nj.com/opinion/times/oped/index.ssf?/base/news-1/127995040084070.xml&coll=5.

Cobb, Kurt. "Ocean Acidification: Why the Climate Change Deniers Don't Want to Talk About It," *Energy Bulletin*, March 14, 2010. www.energybulletin.net/51946.

Daily Telegraph (London). "Sharks Threatened with Extinction," June 25, 2009. www.telegraph.co.uk/earth/earthnews/5627224/Sharks-threatened-with-extinction.html.

Dallas Morning News. "Deepwater Drilling Moratorium Is Essential," editorial, June 25, 2010. www.dallasnews.com/sharedcontent/dws/dn/opinion/editorials/stories/DN-moratorium_27edi.State.Edition1.50a2776.html.

Eilperin, Juliet. "Global Shark Population Threatened," *Seattle Times*, July 1, 2008. http://seattletimes.nwsource.com/html/nationworld/2008026733_sharks01.html.

Environmental Defense Fund. "Oceans of Abundance," 2008. www.edf.org/documents/8795_OceansOfAbundance.pdf.

Halweil, Brian. "Farming Fish for the Future," World Watch Institute, September 2008. www.unbsj.ca/sase/biology/chopinlab/articles/files/2008.09.05.Halweil%202008%20Farming%20Fish%20for%20the%20Future.pdf.

Hari, Johann. "Could We Be the Generation That Runs Out of Fish?," *Independent* (London), June 5, 2009. www.independent.co.uk/opinion/commentators/johann-hari/johann-hari-could-we-be-the-generation-that-runs-out-of-fish-1697247.html.

Howden, Daniel. "The World's Dump: Ocean Garbage from Hawaii to Japan," *Independent* (London), February 6, 2008. www.alternet.org/water/76056.

Jha, Alok. "Fishing Puts a Third of All Oceanic Shark Species at Risk of Extinction," *Guardian* (Manchester, UK), June 25, 2009. www.guardian.co.uk/science/2009/jun/25/sharks-extinction-iucnred-list.

Johnson, Mike. "Wealth, Jobs, the Fishing Industry, and Obama," *American Thinker,* July 2, 2010. www.americanthinker.com/2010/07/wealth_jobs_the_fishing_indust.html.

Kasahara, Katsumi. "Protests or Not, Japan Won't Let Go of Whale Meat," *USA Today,* January 10, 2009. www.usatoday.com/news/world/2009-01-10-japan-whale-meat_N.htm.

Kolbert, Elizabeth. "The Scales Fall: Is There Any Hope for Our Overfished Oceans?," *New Yorker,* August 2, 2010. www.newyorker.com/arts/critics/books/2010/08/02/100802crbo_books_kolbert?currentPage=all.

Learn, Scott. "Reports of Pacific Ocean's Plastic Patch Being Texas-Sized Are Grossly Exaggerated, Oregon State University Professor Says," *Portland Oregonian,* January 4, 2011. www.oregonlive.com/environment/index.ssf/2011/01/reports_of_pacific_oceans_plas.html.

Marsland, Robbie. "We Must Defend the Whaling Ban," *Guardian* (Manchester, UK), August 15, 2008. www.guardian.co.uk/commentisfree/2008/aug/15/conservation.wildlife.

McNally, Jess. "Warming of Oceans Will Reduce and Rearrange Marine Life," *Wired,* July 28, 2010. www.wired.com/wiredscience/2010/07/temperature-ocean-life.

Melia, Mike. "Atlantic Garbage Patch: Pacific Gyre Is Not Alone," *Huffington Post,* April 15, 2010. www.huffingtonpost.com/2010/04/15/atlantic-garbage-patch-pa_n_538514.html.

Morello, Lauren. "Robot Floats Record Sharp Increase in Upper Ocean Warming—Study," *New York Times,* May 20, 2010. www.nytimes.com/cwire/2010/05/20/20climatewire-robot-floats-record-sharp-increase-in-upper-67924.html.

Mörner, Nils-Axel, interviewed by Gregory Murphy. "Claim That Sea Level Is Rising Is a Total Fraud," *Executive Intelligence Review,* June 22, 2007. http://oceanservice.noaa.gov/education/pd/climate/factsheets/issea.pdf.

Morrow, Fiona. "A New Breed of Fish Farming," *Globe and Mail* (Toronto), March 31, 2009. www.theglobeandmail.com/life/article712401.ece.

Natural Resources Defense Council. "Ocean Acidification: The Other CO_2 Problem," September 17, 2009. www.nrdc.org/oceans/acidification/default.asp.

O'Brien, Jeffrey M. "The Wonder Fish," *Fortune,* April 28, 2008.

OzPolitic. "Why We Should Allow Whaling," 2006. www.ozpolitic.com/sustainability-party/why-allow-whaling.html.

Pearce, Fred. "A Total Ban on Whaling? New Studies May Hold the Key," *Yale Environment 360,* July 23, 2009. http://e360.yale.edu/content/feature.msp?id=2173.

People for the Ethical Treatment of Animals. "Stop Carping: Fish Farms Are the Real Problem," *American Chronicle,* February 4, 2010. www.americanchronicle.com/articles/view/140184.

Pew Environment Group. "Sharks: The State of Science," March 26, 2010. www.pewtrusts.org/uploadedFiles/wwwpewtrustsorg/Reports/Protecting_ocean_life/9.%20Pew%20Ocean%20Science%20Sharks%20State%20of%20the%20Science.pdf?n=1381.

Ruder, Eric. "A Nightmare That Only Grows Worse," *Socialist Worker,* May 17, 2010. http://socialistworker.org/2010/05/17/nightmare-only-grows-worse.

Rudolf, John Collins. "An Alert on Ocean Acidity," *New York Times,* December 8, 2010. http://green.blogs.nytimes.com/2010/12/08/an-alert-on-ocean-acidity/?scp=3&sq=oceans&st=cse.

Science Daily. "New Hope for Fisheries: Overfishing Reduced in Several Regions Around the World," July 31, 2009. www.sciencedaily.com/releases/2009/07/090730141555.htm.

Shore, Randy. "New Way of Fish Farming Could Help Fix Environment," *Vancouver (BC) Sun,* March 25, 2010. www.vancouversun.com/technology/fish+farming+could+help+environment/2724153/story.html.

Trenberth, Kevin E. "Global Change: The Ocean Is Warming, Isn't It?," *Nature,* May 19, 2010. www.nature.com/nature/journal/v465/n7296/full/465304a.html.

Websites

Exploratorium (www.exploratorium.edu). Provides scientific data relating to the atmosphere, the oceans, areas covered by ice and snow, and the living organisms in all these domains.

Farmed and Dangerous (www.farmedanddangerous.org). This site is maintained by the Coastal Alliance for Aquaculture Reform. It seeks to protect wild salmon, coastal ecosystems and communities, and human health from what it argues are destructive fish farming practices. Multiple publications on the topic are available for free download.

Mother Nature Network (www.mnn.com). Provides environmental news and information, including regular columns, original articles, blogs, videos, and news from wire services, as well as a section called "Earth Matters," which includes articles and news about marine life.

Overfishing.org (http://overfishing.org). This site provides a wealth of information on fish and the oceans and includes articles, news, discussion forums, and a helpful glossary.

Shark Trust (www.sharktrust.org). This site is run by a British conservation agency. It is dedicated to preserving sharks and their habitat. It contains useful information on the types of sharks and the threats they face as well as many classroom and homework activities on sharks.

Index

A
Abdalati, Waleed, 13
Antarctica
    ice shelf collapse in, is
        isolated, 33–34
    is not melting, 35–36
    West Antarctic Ice Sheet
        melting as driver of rising
        sea levels, 24
    western peninsula, effects of
        ice melt on, *32*
Aquaculture. *See* Fish Farming
Arctic
    increase in water temperature
        near, 12
    reduction of perennial ice in,
        13
Argo monitors, 17, *18*
Arndt, Deke, 13
Atlantic Salmon Watch
    Program (ASWP), 70

B
Babbitt, Bruce, 26
Balsiger, Jim, 62
Blue fin tuna, 52, 54, *75*
Botha, Paul, 8
Boxall, Simon, 80, 81, 82, 85
British Antarctic Survey, 33
British Petroleum (BP) oil spill,
    102, *105*, 108, 111
    Americans' opinions on
        offshore drilling after, *109*

amount of oil involved, 104
    See also Deepwater oil drilling

C
CAAR (Coastal Alliance for
    Aquaculture Reform, 65
Canadian Journal of Fisheries, 69
Carbon dioxide (CO_2)
    changes in atmospheric levels
        are normal, 47
    ocean acidification and, 38,
        41, 44, 45
Cetaceans, effects of noise
    pollution on, 95–96, 98
Christ, Charlie, 106
Cleveland, Cutler, 108
Coastal Alliance for Aquaculture
    Reform (CAAR), 65
Cohen, Kenneth, 106
Conservation Biology (journal),
    70
Coral reefs, effects of
    increased ocean acidity,
        39–41, 46
    warming temperatures, 14–15
CO_2 *See* Carbon dioxide
Cousteau, Jacques, 94
Cumming, Ed, 79
Curie, Marie, 47
Curry, Judith, 13, 15

D
D'Aleo, Joe, 31

Daly, Matthew, 102
Deepwater Horizon explosion (2010), *101*, 109–110
Deepwater oil drilling
   Americans still favor, *109*
   moratorium on, 108–109
   should be banned, 102–106
   should not be banned, 107–111
   See also British Petroleum (BP) oil spill; Deepwater Horizon explosion
Dudley, Bob, 108

E
Eakin, C. Mark, 14
Earle, Sylvia, 84
Ebbesmeyer, Curtis, 82
El Niño, 12, 15
Environmental Defense Fund, 58
Estuarine, Coastal and Shelf Science (journal), 45
Etienne, Jean-Louise, *46*

F
FAO (United Nations Food and Agriculture Organization), 51–52
Feldman, Martin, 110
Fish farming
   growth in, 74
   need not threaten ocean fish stocks, 73–78
   number of salmon escapes from, *71*
   threatens ocean fish stocks, 65–72
   top species in, *77*
   world production of, *76*
   See also Salmon farming
Fisheries
   fish farming is threat to, 65–72
   fish farming need not threaten, 73–78
   impact of increased ocean acidity on, 37–42
   status of, *54, 61*
Fisheries Magazine, 63
Fishing
   number of people depending on, for livelihood globally, 118
   See also Overfishing
Franklin, James, 15
Fredrikson, John, *77*

G
Gaffney, Rick, 8
Giacalone, Vito, 62
Great Pacific Garbage Patch (Pacific Trash Vortex), 80, 87–88
   early prediction of, 82
   effect of ocean currents on, *83*
Gulf of Mexico
   average water temperature, 12
   dead zones in, 55
   moratorium on deepwater drilling in, 103–106, 108–111
   percentage of oil reserves in deep water of, 108
   See also British Petroleum (BP) oil spill; Deepwater Horizon explosion

Gutner, Lorne, 16

H
Hastings, Doc, 104
Hayward, Tony, 108
Hilborn, Ray, 63, 119
Hocevar, John, 112
Hornbeck Offshore Services, 110
Hoshaw, Lindsay, 88
Hurricanes, 15

I
Infectious salmon anemia (ISA), 69
Intergovernmental Panel on Climate Change (IPCC), *23*, 24, 26, 45, 47
  prediction on rise in sea levels, 34, 35
  sea level calculations of, 22
International Fund for Animal Welfare, 93
International Union for Conservation of Nature, 55
IPCC. *See* Intergovernmental Panel on Climate Change

J
Jindal, Bobby, 104, *110*

K
Ketten, Darlene R., 97
Kramer, Steve, 12
Krill, 51, 76

L
Libya, oil reserves of, 111

Lovgren, James, 62–63
Lubchenco, Jane, 58, 59

M
Marine Life Protection Act (CA, 1999), 118
Marine mammals, noise pollution is serious threat to, 93–100
McDonnell, Robert, 104
Menendez, Robert, 106
Ministry of Agriculture and Lands (British Columbia), 70–71, 74
Mississippi Delta, sea level rise and, 26
Moore, Charles, 82
Mörner, Nils-Axel, 33
Murawski, Steven, 60, 62, 64

N
National Aeronautics and Space Administration (NASA), 19
National Climatic Data Center, 12
National Oceanic and Atmospheric Administration (NOAA), 19, 113
Natural Resources Defense Council (NRDC), 37
Nature (journal), 38, 63
Newman, Steve, 109–110
Nies, Tom, 60
NOAA (National Oceanic and Atmospheric Administration), 19, 113
Norwegian Polar Institute (NPI), 31, 32–33

Nøst, Ole Anders, 33
NRDC (Natural Resources
    Defense Council), 37

O
Obama, Barack/Obama
    administration, 58, 103
Ocean acidification
    fish biomass in attenuation
        of, 55
    is dangerous threat to oceans/
        sea life, 37–42
    predicted level of, 38
    process of, *40*
    as threat is exaggerated, 43–48
Ocean Voyages Institute, 87–88
Ocean(s)
    are cooling, 16–20
    are warming, 11–15
    levels are not rising, 30–36
    levels are rising, 21–29
    overfishing as threat to, is
        exaggerated, 57–64
    overfishing is serious threat
        to, 50–56
    pH of, *39*
    plastic waste as threat is
        exaggerated, 86–92
    plastic waste is serious threat
        to, 79–85
    ship traffic on, 94, *95*
    trend in global average sea
        level in, *27*
Oceans of Abundance
    (Environmental Defense
    Fund), 58–59
Offshore oil drilling. *See*
    Deepwater oil drilling

Oil drilling. *See* Deepwater oil
    drilling
Opinion polls. *See* Surveys
Ouellette, Stephen, 60
Overfishing, *53*
    crisis in, is a myth, 117–121
    is serious threat to oceans,
        50–56, *54*
    protection of fish populations
        will solve crisis in, 112–116

P
Pacific Trash Vortex. *See* Great
    Pacific Garbage Patch
Pauly, Daniel, 50, 58
pH scale, *39*, 44–45
Pilkey, Orrin, 21
Plankton, 82, 88, 89
Plastic waste, *49*, *91*
    is serious threat to oceans,
        79–85
    as threat to oceans is
        exaggerated, 86–92
Plastiki (catamaran), 80, *81*
Polls. *See* Surveys
Project Karesi, 87, 88
Pryor, Jay, 110

Q
Quinn, Jennifer, 107

R
The Rising Sea (Young and
    Pilkey), 23
Robbins, Martin, 86
Rothschild, Brian, 61–62, 64
Rothschild, David de, 80
Royle, Jo, 82–83, 84, 85
Rutzen, Mike, 7–8

S
Salazar, Ken, 103, 104
Salmon farming, 66
    number of fish escaping from,
        71
    as threat to wild salmon
        populations, 69–71,76–77
    See also Sea lice
Santillo, David, 87
Savitz, Jacqueline, 106
Science (journal), 58, 63
Sea level
    global average, trend in, 27
    impacts of rise in, 24–26,
        26–28
    predicted rise in, 26
Sea lice, 66, 67–69, 76–77
    salmon fry infested with, 68
Sea turtles, 103
    threats to, 113
Seawater, pH of, 39
Shark tourism, 7–8
Shark Trust, 8
Sharks, threats to, 7, 55
Sheppard, Marc, 30
Snow cover, in northern
    hemisphere, 27
Suatoni, Lisa, 41
Surveys
    on concern over rising sea
        levels, 25
    on offshore drilling after BP
        oil spill, 109
Suzuki, David, 88

T
Temperature
    average global, trend in, 27

global and continental,
    changes in, 14
ocean, average global, 12
Tripp, Tom, 47

U
United Nations Environment
    Program, 80, 82
United Nations Fish and
    Agriculture Organization,
    118
United Nations Food and
    Agriculture Organization
    (FAO), 51–52

W
Wardell, Jane, 107
Warner, Mark, 104
Weaver, Andrew, 13
Westwell, Steve, 111
Whales
    effects of sonar testing on,
        98–99
    sounds of, 96–97
White, Angelicque, 88
Whitley, Mary Ann, 11
Willis, Josh, 18, 19
World Bank, 54
World Wildlife Federation,
    8
Worm, Boris, 58, 63–64,
    119

Y
Young, Rob, 21

Z
Zhu, John, 88–89

Picture Credits

© Alaska Stock LLC/Alamy, 115
ANT Photo Library/Photo Researchers, Inc., 91
Don Arnold/Wire Image/Getty Images, 81
Noah Berger/AP Images, 120
Michael Democker/The Times-Picayune/Landov, 101
Neil Eliot/AP Images, 97
Long Fu/Color China Photo/AP Images, 53
Mario Garcia/NBC NewsWire via AP Images, 10
Eric Gay/AP Images, 103
Kyodo/Landov, 75
Richard Lam/AP Images, 68
Frances Latrielle, Septieme Continent/AP Images, 46
Maurice McDonald/AP Images, 59
NASA/AP Images, 13
NOAA, Ed Lyman/AP Images, 49
Reuters/Landov, 32, 40
Charlie Riedel/AP Images, 110
Lalo R. Villar/AP Images, 18
Roger L. Wollenberg/UPI/Landov, 23
Steve Zmina, 14, 25, 27, 39, 54, 61, 71, 76, 77, 83, 95, 105, 109